# Foreword

This report discusses contemporary developments in public sector leadership. It covers six OECD Member countries: the United Kingdom, the United States, Germany, Sweden, Norway and Mexico. These case studies were presented to the OECD Human Resources Management Working Party meeting held in Paris on 3-4 July 2000.

This report was produced by the OECD Public Management Service (PUMA). Deok-Seob Shim edited the report; he and Alex Matheson wrote the overview chapter. Hélène Leconte, Jennifer Gardner and Marie Murphy provided the technical support. The editor would like to thank the following contributors to the case studies: Malcolm Dawson, Barbara Garvin-Kester, Joachim Vollmuth, Monica Wåglund, Finn Melbø, Turid Semb, and Luis Guillermo Ibarra. This report is published on the responsibility of the Secretary-General of OECD.

# Table of Contents

# Public Sector Leadership for the 21st Century

OECD

ORGANISATION FOR ECONOMIC CO-OPERATION AND DEVELOPMENT

# ORGANISATION FOR ECONOMIC CO-OPERATION AND DEVELOPMENT

Pursuant to Article 1 of the Convention signed in Paris on 14th December 1960, and which came into force on 30th September 1961, the Organisation for Economic Co-operation and Development (OECD) shall promote policies designed:

- to achieve the highest sustainable economic growth and employment and a rising standard of living in Member countries, while maintaining financial stability, and thus to contribute to the development of the world economy;
- to contribute to sound economic expansion in Member as well as non-member countries in the process of economic development; and
- to contribute to the expansion of world trade on a multilateral, non-discriminatory basis in accordance with international obligations.

The original Member countries of the OECD are Austria, Belgium, Canada, Denmark, France, Germany, Greece, Iceland, Ireland, Italy, Luxembourg, the Netherlands, Norway, Portugal, Spain, Sweden, Switzerland, Turkey, the United Kingdom and the United States. The following countries became Members subsequently through accession at the dates indicated hereafter: Japan (28th April 1964), Finland (28th January 1969), Australia (7th June 1971), New Zealand (29th May 1973), Mexico (18th May 1994), the Czech Republic (21st December 1995), Hungary (7th May 1996), Poland (22nd November 1996), Korea (12th December 1996) and the Slovak Republic (14th December 2000). The Commission of the European Communities takes part in the work of the OECD (Article 13 of the OECD Convention).

*Publié en français sous le titre :*
LE SECTEUR PUBLIC AU XXI<sup>e</sup> SIÈCLE : REPENSER LE LEADERSHIP

# Executive Summary

Leadership development is neither new nor unique to the public sector. Why then has it become a hot issue? In general, OECD Member countries are finding that there is a gap between how their public sectors are, and how the interests of the nation need them to be now or in the future. Member countries are finding something missing between existing public service cultures and the public interest. A common complaint is lack of dedication to the underlying values of public service and the interests of the citizens served. A common response seems to be the attempt to promote a certain kind of leadership.

Leadership is a critical component of *good public governance*, which is a major theme for current OECD work. Governance can be briefly described as the way in which the underlying values of a nation (usually articulated in some way in its Constitution) are "institutionalised". This has formal aspects such as separated powers, checks and balances, means of transferring power, transparency, and accountability. However, for these values to be actualised, they must guide the actions of public officials throughout the system. They must be imbedded in culture. In this regard "leadership" is the flesh on the bones of the Constitution. It is at the heart of good governance.

The most important role of public sector leaders has been to solve the problems and challenges faced in a specific environment. When we say we want more leadership in the public sector, what we are really looking for is *people who will promote institutional adaptations in the public interest*. Leadership in this sense is not value neutral. It is a positive espousal of the need to promote certain fundamental values that can be called *public spiritedness*.

Leadership is an important and crucial variable that leads to enhanced management capacity, as well as organisational performance. A leadership focus also plays an integrating role among various Human Resource Management components including recruitment and selection, training and development, performance management, public service ethics, and succession planning.

The leadership development strategies of OECD Member countries, histori-cally and culturally are spread across a wide spectrum. At one end is a high level of central intervention in which future leaders are identified and nurtured from the early stage through a centralised selection, training and career management process. In contrast there is a growing group of countries which adopt "market-type" approaches to developing and securing leaders. Between these poles, there are different mixes of the two approaches. Many countries now have designated "Senior Executive Services" membership – with varying degrees of central intervention.

General trends of leadership development in OECD Member countries are:

- *Developing comprehensive strategies*: A few countries have set up systematic strategies for leadership development. For instance, the UK Government has recently started to work on a leadership development model. The Norwegian Government has renewed its strategic plan for leadership in the civil service, in order to reflect increased concern for public sector change.

- *Setting up new institutions for leadership development*: In some countries, like Sweden and the US, governments have set up new institutions for identifying and developing future leaders in the public sector. In Sweden, the National Council for Quality and Development was created recently with the main task of identifying potential leaders.

- *Linking the existing management training to leadership development*: Many countries are expanding their existing management development programmes to encompass leadership development. One leadership development programme in Finland includes the creation of a new management development programme following re-evaluation of their previous one.

There is no single best model for developing future leaders, because each country has its unique public sector values to be emphasised and the management systems are different from country to country. Despite the diversity of strategies and approaches adopted by OECD Member countries, some general and common trends in developing future leaders can be drawn from the country experiences:

- *To define a competence profile for future leaders*: In the UK and the US, the first step taken to develop future leaders was to define the competence profile for future leaders. The idea underlying this is that competencies required for future leaders could be different from those required for present leaders in terms of their responsibility, capability, and role. For this reason, it is essential to predict what forms the future public sector will take, and what challenges will be faced in order to identify and develop leaders suitable for the future environment.

- *To identify and select potential leaders*: Given the competence framework for future leaders, the next step is often to identify and select potential future leaders. This issue involves the choice of whether to select future leaders from outside or to nurture them within the public sector. If a country puts more emphasis on the former method rather than the latter, it should also address the question of how to recruit "the best and the brightest" candidates in competing with other sectors.

- *To encourage mentoring and training*: Once potential leaders are identified and selected, the next step is to train them continuously. For this purpose, some countries set up a specialised institution for leadership development. Others put greater emphasis on leadership in existing curricula and establish new training courses for the top executives or senior managers.

- *To keep leadership development sustainable*: As developing future leaders takes a long time, it is very important to keep the leadership development sustainable. To do so, developing a comprehensive programme from the whole-of-government perspective is essential for developing future leaders. Allocating more of managers' time to developing leaders, and linking incentives with performance for better leadership are crucial to the success of leadership development programmes.

From the country experiences, we have noticed some pitfalls of the leadership development strategies, to which special attention should be paid. First of all, developing an elite leadership cadre has many advantages. However, there are some possible dangers in developing leadership in this way. If a group of leaders begins to pursue their own interests rather than the national interest, the country may suffer. Such a group may become closed and insufficiently responsive to wider changes in society. So, new issues on the agenda are how to build a leadership cadre that is more responsive or representative, and also, how to re-orient and refresh existing cadres if they have begun to get out of step with the society they represent.

Secondly, many Member countries are looking to the strengthening of leadership as the solution to national public challenges. How they approach leadership however needs to be viewed in the context of the kinds of problems being faced. It seems important for leadership strategies to be based on a clear diagnosis of the national challenges being faced, and the current characteristics of the public sector culture – pursuing "leadership" development without that diagnosis and strategy is likely to be ineffective.

Thirdly, any successful leadership strategy involves culture change. We know both that culture change is very difficult, and that where it does take place it is over a long period and in response to a variety of powerful pressures. In strengthening OECD efforts in this area it is clear that we need better quality information on the degree to which past public sector leadership promotion strategies have actually changed behaviour. On this basis, countries will be better placed to diagnose the current problem and formulate strategies which are likely to be effective.

Chapter 1

# Developing Public Sector Leadership for the 21st Century

## 1. Introduction

This chapter proposes a way of thinking about public sector leadership. It describes various leadership development strategies adopted in OECD Member countries, it draws some strategic lessons learned from the country cases and, finally, it outlines areas which need future work. It is based mainly on the OECD Member countries' practical experience that was presented to the OECD Human Resources Management (HRM) Working Party meeting held in July 2000. It also refers to the results of PUMA's survey conducted in June 2000 on recent HRM developments in OECD Member countries.

### Leadership as a concept

Leadership means a variety of things. Sometimes it refers to the possession of personal properties such as courage, stamina, or charisma. At other times, it means a property of a position which dispenses power, authority, and responsibility. A review of literature on leadership suggests as many definitions of leadership as there are scholars who have attempted to define it. Perhaps the closest to a consensus definition of leadership is that of *social influence process*, although the same may be said for most experiences that involve more than one person.

The Public Management Service (PUMA) has been asked by Member countries to work on leadership. We take the position that the core of leadership is how individuals influence others, particularly in respect to accessing their *inner* motivation. Leaders appeal because those who follow them believe that their values and deeper interests are served by so doing. Although not a clear-cut distinction, leadership differs from management in so far as the latter tends to be about more tangible incentives on behaviour.

But of course leaders can be good or bad, and the attributes of leadership can be used in support of, or contrary to the public interest. We have assumed that our Members countries governments are not interested in a treatise on leadership in this amoral sense.

11

### What is the problem?

So we have instead asked *what is the problem that Member countries are facing to which they hope leadership may be the answer?* In general Member countries are finding there is a gap between how their public sectors are now, and how the interests of the nation needs them to be now or in the future. In all countries structural and management reform in the public sector has been used to better align public services with the needs of contemporary society. But, both in trying to make these reforms and in how things are after such reforms, Member countries are finding something missing between existing public service cultures and the public interest. What is it? A common complaint is lack of dedication to the underlying values of public service and the interests of the citizens served. How to fix it? A common conclusion seems to be by promoting a certain kind of leadership.

### Our definition

We therefore define the public sector leadership problem in a normative way.

*How to develop more public officials who can draw others into a strong spirit of public service geared to the needs of contemporary society, and thereby make their services to government and to citizens more effective?*

In addressing this problem we are not assuming that leadership comes only from those in positions of formal authority. Our study pays special attention to this senior group, but it also recognises that officials at all levels exert influence on others. For this reason, this study is about the development of *leadership*, including, but not confined to, development of *leaders*.

### Leadership and governance

Leadership is a critical component of *good public governance*, which is a major theme for current OECD work. Governance can be briefly described as the way in which the underlying values of a nation (usually articulated in some way in its Constitution) are "institutionalised". This has formal aspects such as separated powers, checks and balances, means of transferring power, transparency, and accountability. However for these values to be actualised, they must guide the actions of public officials throughout the system – they must be imbedded in culture. In this regard "leadership" in the sense we have defined, is the flesh on the bones of the Constitution. It is at the heart of good governance.

### 2. Why Leadership Now?

The concept of leadership is neither new nor unique to the public sector. It has been discussed frequently in the public management, as well as business management, literature. It seems, however, that interest in public sector leadership development has had a resurgence in recent years. An OECD Survey shows that many OECD governments, including Germany, Iceland, New Zealand, Norway, the UK, and the US, have given high priority to this issue during the last couple of years.

There are various reasons for leadership development becoming a more important issue in OECD Member countries. Part of it seems to be the effort to drive reform. The British Government cites stronger leadership as one of the six key themes for civil service reform. With the growing interest in public service accountability and co-operation, the New Zealand Government stresses the importance of leadership to foster these ideals. In general, there seem to be at least four reasons for the growing attention to leadership.

## *Changing environment requires a new type of leadership...*

Globalisation, decentralisation, and more intensive use of IT are some key elements for government in the new century. Globalisation of economic and social policies creates a need for new capacities to exploit new opportunities to deal with international implications of policy issues. At the same time, greater decentralisation of national policy is increasing fragmentation of policy responsibilities, posing major challenges of policy co-ordination, accountability, and coherence. Rapid development of information and technology gives the potential for governments to cope with new problems in a swift, transparent and flexible manner. In order to effectively cope with a variety of dynamic demands such as aggressive competition, employee needs, market demands, IT advances, and global economic shifts, new approaches to leadership are required, which are better fitted for the tasks of redesigning, renovating or reinventing existing organisations, as well as securing coherence, accountability, and co-ordination among policies and various interests.

Within this changing environment, OECD Member countries are placing more emphasis on leadership because:

- The growing need for people to think and act global and local requires leaders to pay more attention to policy coherence. In particular the shift of power between citizens and government has increased the importance of leadership in the public service and has made the task of managers more demanding.

- In many OECD Member countries the attractions of work in the private sector and other parts of society seem to be increasing at the expense of the public service, and there is an increasing need for many countries to take a new look at how to ensure they have leaders and managers of the right quality.

13

- In a knowledge-intensive economy, government needs to increase the knowledge basis of their activities and keep track and integrate knowledge as it is increasingly produced. This calls for a new type of leadership that inspires others to create and share knowledge.

- Finally, our external environment is changing fast and there is a continuing need for public sector organisations to make very serious adaptations if they are to continue to be useful. In practical terms this situation puts greater demands on leadership – not just amongst senior managers, but amongst all public officials, elected and appointed.

### Leadership focus is changing...

Truly effective leaders in any age have always been more subtle, but the traditional paradigm of leadership is strongly that of command and control in which there is a clear distinction of roles of leaders and followers. Under this model, the relationship between leaders and followers is based firmly on the leaders' authority, and the subservience of the followers to that authority.

However, in a decentralised, knowledge-intensive, and "webbed" society, this classical leadership model is losing ground. Relationships between leaders and followers have been changing.

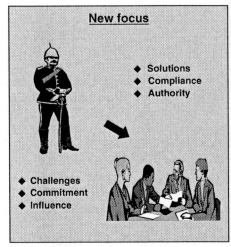

Source: OECD.

Authority is no longer as complete as it used to be, hierarchies have been lowered in many organisations, and because of a range of social changes, including more mobility and job opportunity, today's public sector leaders need to get *commitment* from their followers, not just their *compliance*. As a result, today's leaders have to find ways beyond their authority to influence their followers effectively.

### Leadership differs from management...

"Leadership" and "Management" are often used interchangeably. In practice, the two concepts overlap heavily. They share many common features in that both are based on institutional structures and systems, and both are oriented towards better performance of the organisation. But they do represent a difference in emphasis. According to Jo Brosnahan,[1] leadership means paying more attention to the development of attributes that focus on integrity, vision, the ability to inspire others, awareness of self, courage to innovate, and judgement. While management puts more emphasis on formal systems, processes and incentives, leadership is more about informal influence – how to mobilise people through values and visions.

As hierarchies are being reduced and information and technology is developing, the public sector environment requires some competencies different from the conventional management ones. Governments are finding that managerial skills and qualities that had been given importance during the last two decades or so are not sufficient to cope with future challenges. Hence the effort to re-identify skills and qualities required for public sector leaders. From the country cases, these components of public sector leadership requiring more emphasis are:

- focusing on delivery of results;
- challenging assumptions;
- being open to learning from outside;
- understanding the environment and its impact;
- thinking and acting strategically;
- building new patterns and ways of working;
- developing and communicating a personal vision of change.

## New leadership involves all levels...

In the traditional leadership hierarchy, leaders were considered to be those very few people in higher positions within the hierarchy. But in the new leadership model, leadership involves all levels though their roles are different from each other. The US Government identifies three different types of leadership in the hierarchy; *strategic leadership, team leadership, and technical leadership.*

- *Strategic leadership* is required at the higher levels for such components as strategic thinking, political savvy, vision, external awareness, influencing or negotiating, and cultural awareness.

- In the middle level, *team leadership* is more important than others, with team building and interpersonal skills as crucial competencies.

- The lower level employees need *technical leadership*, emphasising professional and technical skills.

The idea of leadership being required at all levels is revolutionary in its potential impact, and is an important driver of the move to redefine public sector leadership.

15

### 3. The role of leadership

*Change/reform agents*

Throughout time, the most important role of public sector leaders has been to solve the problems and challenges faced in a specific environment. What then is the problem that we need the present leadership to solve? Heifetz[2] argues that it is the problem of adaptation. By adaptation, however, he does not mean just coping. He is talking about the capacity to promote adaptations which will further restore and promote the fundamental interests and values of the society or organisation in question in circumstances when there is a big gap between how things are and how they should be. To put it in public sector terms, the problem is how can nations, governments and public agencies adapt to changing circumstances when the changes required are beyond the scope of existing ways of doing things?

Heifetz takes the view that when people come under severe stress because of a gap between how things are and how they would like them to be, they have two equally dysfunctional tendencies.

- One is to look for some person or organisation to blame for the stress – to create a "scapegoat". It simplifies the problem and allows an outlet for the stress – is the IMF, for instance, really responsible for the huge changes being wrought by globalisation?

- The other is to look to some individual as their saviour – to place undue faith in the capacity of a particular individual to "lead" them out of the difficulties. Dictators almost always come to power in a period of national stress when people desperately want someone to solve their problems for them.

Following this analysis, when we say we want more leadership in the public sector, what we are really looking for is *people who will promote institutional adaptations in the public interest*. Leadership in this sense is not value neutral. It is a positive espousal of the need to promote certain fundamental values that can be called *public spiritedness*.

In particular, leadership plays an important role in the implementation of public sector reform because it involves two of the most important aspects of reform: *change* and *people*. Leadership is manifested in relations between people. Good leaders inspire people. Changing organisations is really about changing people's behaviour; so organisations undergoing reform need leadership. Leaders, spread throughout an organisation, can help to diffuse and maintain the new values that are necessary for successful public sector reform. Instead of being all-powerful authority figures, leaders in the future will need to be able to persuade people and to focus their efforts on a common cause.

## Enhancing organisational capacity/performance

Leadership is an important and crucial variable that leads to enhanced management capacity as well as organisational performance. Figure I maps out the hypothetical relationships between leadership and organisational performance. Within a given organisational culture, how leadership is exercised largely determines the level of management capacity, by mobilising the use of available resources such as manpower, money, and information, etc., and by affecting various management systems like HR management, budgeting systems, institutional arrangement, and IT, etc. Enhanced management capacity, however, does not necessarily lead to higher organisational performance. Management capacity should be used for achieving organisational performance. To do this, the steering role of leaders is very important in achieving the performance target. Organisational culture affects this process directly or indirectly, sometimes as an accelerator or sometimes as an obstacle.

In this light, leadership plays a significant role in achieving both enhanced management capacity and organisational performance. But there has been no particular empirical study that explores the relationships so far. It is one of the key areas to be investigated in future leadership studies.

Figure 1.   **Leadership and Management Capacity/Performance**

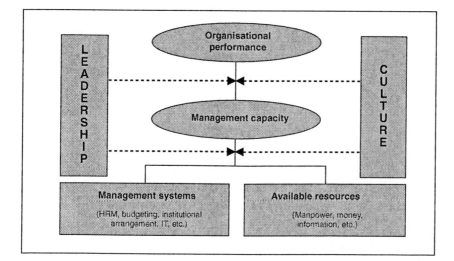

In measuring organisational performance, focus has recently shifted in a couple of countries from outputs to outcomes. This goes along with a necessary change in civil service culture. It is not the outputs but rather the impact on society that really matters, which opens up the horizon to more complex and cross-cutting issues. Leadership is essential to support the cultural change thereof, communicate the new society-wide focus, motivate the staff for this task and facilitate co-operation across departmental boundaries. This outcome-oriented framework usually gives organisations a high degree of freedom and flexibility to contribute to the outcomes. Leaders must be able to use this flexibility, motivate their staff and provide them with appropriate incentives to fulfil the mission. Eventually, the leaders (or sometimes managers) will be held accountable for the outputs of their agencies.

## Integrating other HRM activities

Leadership constitutes an important component of human resources management. It also plays an integrating role among various HRM components. The first and most crucial stage in the development of leadership is the selection of leaders, because when wrong persons are selected, there is little use in developing them. It is essential to define the skills and competencies that future leaders should have. On the basis of this, the selection procedure should ensure applicants with the best competencies as well as a strong desire to work with people be appointed. In this regard, leadership competencies need to be tested thoroughly. As can be seen in Figure 2, leadership development is closely connected with each of the HRM activities in the personnel management cycle.

There is a particularly close relationship between public sector leadership and public service ethics. Normatively, the public sector leaders should demonstrate high ethical standards of transparency and accountability. In addition, their role as promoters of high standards of public service in general is becoming more important because public service ethics are a prerequisite to, and underpin, public trust, and are a keystone of good governance.

## Leadership role differs in different context

The degree of importance attributed to developing public sector leadership differs considerably from country to country. At the OECD Symposium on Government of the Future in 1999, delegates indicated that the importance of leadership largely depends on the make-up of the society, the structure of the organisation and the type of reform.[3]

- Developing leaders is more important in a diversified society than in a homogenous society, because leaders are required to transmit new values, mediate differences, and create coalitions in support of reform.

Figure 2. **Leadership in the HRM cycle**

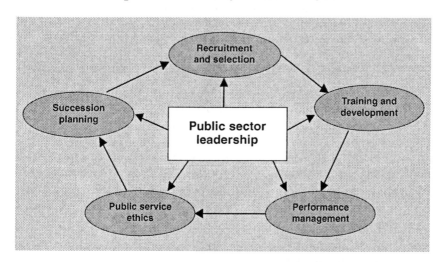

*Source:* OECD.

- Leadership is more important in a decentralised and "webbed" govern-ment than in a hierarchical and rule-based government.
- Countries that have chosen a path of incremental reform will be less likely to mobilise many leaders at once. However, where reform is greater and more widespread, there is a higher premium placed on leadership.

## 4. Leadership development strategies in OECD Member countries

### General trends in OECD Member countries

Historically and culturally, OECD Member countries are spread across a wide spectrum in their strategies for developing their public sector leaders. At one end of the spectrum is a high level of central intervention in which future leaders are identified and nurtured from the early stage through a centralised selection, training and career management process. The most salient case can be found in the *École Nationale d'Administration* (ENA) of France. This school has played an overwhelming role in creating the French administrative elite. The top 20% of graduates, ranked according to performance, are automatically guaranteed jobs in the five elite grand corps of the French civil service, including the *Inspection des Finances* and the *Cours des Comptes*, or auditors office. East Asian countries like Japan and Korea have a similar strategy. They select potential leaders through special exams, and nurture them from an early stage.

In contrast, at the other end of the spectrum there is a growing group of countries which adopt "market-type" approaches to developing and securing leaders. In the purest form of this (of which New Zealand is perhaps a good example), there is a very light co-ordinating role at the centre, all senior posts are widely advertised and can in theory be awarded to anyone who meets the skill and knowledge requirements.

Between these poles, there are different mixes of the two approaches. Many countries have now designated "Senior Executive Services" membership – with varying degrees of central intervention. Some countries are introducing more market into centralised elite systems because the elite can over time become unresponsive to social change. In the other extreme, some countries are finding that highly market driven systems create difficulties in forming an adequate pool from which they can recruit for key public sector positions, and may undermine the development of a set of collective values to bind the public sector together.

In most OECD Member countries, control of leadership is held at central government level but there is considerable flexibility within departments and agencies to adapt leadership strategies according to their particular needs. General trends of leadership development in OECD Member countries can be summarised as follows.

### Developing comprehensive strategies

According to the survey results, there are only a few countries that set up systematic strategies for leadership development. For instance, the UK Government has recently started to work on a leadership development model. The Norwegian Government has renewed its strategic plan for leadership in the civil service, in order to reflect increased concern for public sector change.

### Setting up new institutions for leadership development

In some countries, like Sweden and the US, governments have set up new institutions for identifying and developing future leaders in the public sector. In Sweden, the National Council for Quality and Development was created recently with the main task of identifying potential leaders.

### Linking the existing management training to leadership development

Meanwhile, many countries tend to expand their existing management development programmes to encompass leadership development. One leadership development programme in Finland includes the creation of a new management development programme following re-evaluation of their previous one. In the Netherlands, the Senior Public Service was expanded to include all senior management to cope with the increasing need for a larger number of executive leaders.

## Country case studies

### United Kingdom

In the United Kingdom, the Civil Service has been undergoing major reform since 1999, which is expected to take from three to five years. The Cabinet Office is in the process of defining the leadership skills required for the 21st century, in order to establish programmes to ensure that these skills are obtained, and maintained. To this end, two projects have been instituted with the aim of defining leadership: *i)* identify a set of core competencies; and *ii)* the Senior Civil Service Leadership Project. Leadership seminars and workshops attended by most senior civil servants have been conducted in order to canvass opinion and establish the parameters of these projects. The 21st century Senior Civil Servant needs to acquire new skills; he or she must have the insight and the skills to communicate the broader vision, be receptive and responsive to staff, and open to change and learning.

### United States

Leadership development in the United States has been supervised by the Office of Personnel Management (OPM), established over 20 years ago. One of their first strategies was to draw up a list of Executive Core Qualifications (ECQs) which are continually monitored and adjusted to suit current requirements. Training schemes are based on these ECQs, which are designed to foster creative thinking, the ability to negotiate, relate with staff, handle increasingly complex information technology, improve business acumen, and aid in recognising particular talents amongst staff, etc. The OPM established the Office of Executive and Management Development (OEMD) to organise assessment programmes, training seminars and continuous learning opportunities. The OEMD also engages in partnerships with agencies and departments within the Federal Administration to examine and improve leadership skills according to their specific requirements. Another division, the Office of Resource Management, also offers leadership symposia and seminars for networking and exchanging ideas.

### Germany

In the aim of providing a more efficient and citizen-oriented civil service, almost all ministries and departments in the German Federal Administration have formulated their own strategies to develop and improve leadership. Newcomers to the civil service take part in compulsory introduction and induction programmes organised by the Federal Academy for Public Administration. This academy was established in 1968 for the precise purpose of training staff in the higher civil service. It also offers ongoing training during the first three years of

21

appointment. The German public administration of today also favours generalists, and increasingly needs leaders with international skills and competence in European matters. Control of leadership is by performance dialogues at least once a year, established evaluation criteria for appointment and advancement, and a new technique introduced recently: evaluation of performance by one's own staff. The latter technique was recommended by a working group set up by the federal government to manage the development and implementation of leadership programmes for the future.

*Sweden*

In Sweden most of the recruitment decisions and management training are handled by agency managers. This provides greater flexibility to the individual departments in their staff policies, but central government maintains its control by appointing those who manage the agencies. It also maintains control in its formal recruitment policy, adopted in the mid-1990s, which identified six key aspects:

- **Professional recruitment:** each position requires a written schedule, and candidates are sought from the business sector, and from municipalities and county councils, as well as from government.

- **More women in managerial positions:** it recommends the inclusion of female candidates in shortlists.

- **Good induction programmes:** considerable attention is given to induction programmes in the Swedish public administration, organised both individually for new appointments as well as in groups.

- **Continuous development of managers' skills:** leadership training is provided both for new and experienced managers. Group sessions allow managers to share and resolve issues with colleagues.

- **Performance dialogues:** these are held annually between the agency head and the ministry responsible for his appointment.

- **Mobility between appointments:** this is regarded as an advantage and is encouraged by appointments for limited periods. The manager with wider experience brings additional skills to his department.

In 1999, the Swedish Government set up the National Council for Quality and Development, a body responsible for overall control of management in agencies and public administration, which offers a range of management training programmes. Amongst these is a programme for female managers and a mentor programme which has proved particularly popular.

*Norway*

The Directorate of Public Management, which is a subordinate agency of the Ministry of Labour and Government Administration, holds the main responsibility for leadership development in Norway and has recently prepared a detailed strategy for managers and management. This also acknowledges the greater skills and demands required of the leader in this technologically advanced and more diverse society. Ongoing training of managers is recognised as being as important as initial training, and the manager of today is supported by seminars and workshops to aid in relating to staff, and to acquire skills in encouraging teamwork, vision and incentive. Increasing representation of women in management is also regarded as a priority. The strategy covers the period 1998-2002 and will see the implementation of improved leadership training schemes.

*Mexico*

Recent and major reform in the Mexican Civil Service recognises the importance of training leaders suitable for a more efficient and people-oriented administration. This will institute recruitment policies which were previously non-existent as well as professional development programmes and performance appraisals. A compulsory training scheme for civil servants was introduced in July 2000. The Civil Service Unit (USC) within the Ministry of Finance has set up a Directive Committee on Quality, and an Executive Committee on Quality, both designed to improve the performance of leaders of the USC and to ensure that the wider society receives the services it requires.

## 5. Common steps taken for developing future leaders

The survey shows that OECD Member countries have taken a variety of approaches for developing their public sector leaders. But there is no single best model for developing future leaders, because each country has its unique public sector values to be emphasised and the management systems are different from country to country. Despite the diversity of strategies and approaches adopted by Member countries, some general and common trends in developing future leaders can be drawn from the country experiences, although they are not exhaustive.

### To define a competence profile for future leaders

In the UK and the US, the first step taken to develop future leaders was to define the competence profile for future leaders. The idea underlying this is that competencies required for future leaders could be different from those required for present leaders in terms of their responsibility, capability and role. For this reason, it is essential to predict what form the future public sector will take, and what challenges will be faced in order to identify and develop leaders suitable for the future environment.

For this purpose, the UK Civil Service has produced the new Senior Civil Service (SCS) core competence framework which aims to reflect better the more diverse, creative, strategic and people-centred organisation. The framework structure is shown in Table 1. The developed draft of this competence framework has been validated through extensive survey, workshops and benchmarking against good practices. The competence framework was launched in April 2001 as part of a new SCS performance management and pay system which focuses on training and development needs and career planning as well as providing incentives for good performance and *delivery of results*.

Table 1. **Senior Civil Service Competence Framework-Leadership for Results**

| Giving Purpose and Direction *Creating and communicating a vision of the future* | Making a Personal Impact *Leading by example* | Thinking Strategically *Harnessing ideas and opportunities to achieve goals* |
|---|---|---|
| Getting the Best from People *Motivating and developing people to achieve high performance* | Learning and Improving *Drawing on experience and new ideas to improve results* | Focusing on Delivery *Achieving value for money and results* |

*Source*: OECD.

The US Government has also developed and defined a set of key characteristics and leadership competencies, called Executive Core Qualifications (ECQs). The US ECQs and their 27 components are listed in Table 2. These ECQs are used to: *i*) identify developmental needs of individuals; *ii*) select and certify candidates for the Senior Executive Service (SES), which is the most senior level in the US; and *iii*) measure performance in the first year of service of these newly-appointed leaders.

The Finnish Government also revised its selection criteria for top government officials in 1997. The goal of the revised criteria is to transform the role of top officials to cope with globalisation and changes in government, especially those that have increased the authority and responsibility of governmental departments and agencies. The new selection criteria seek to improve the competence of top managers through *statutory* qualifications and *general* qualifications. The *statutory* or job specific qualifications include higher academic degrees, relevant policy expertise and proven management ability and, at the highest level of government top management experience. *General* qualifications, or those rules that apply to all

Table 2.  **ECQs and 27 Components**

| ECQs | Components | |
|---|---|---|
| Leading Change | • Continual Learning<br>• Creativity and Innovation<br>• External Awareness<br>• Flexibility | • Resilience<br>• Service Motivation<br>• Strategic Thinking<br>• Vision |
| Leading People | • Conflict Management<br>• Cultural Awareness | • Integrity/Honesty<br>• Team Building |
| Results Driven | • Accountability<br>• Customer Service<br>• Decisiveness | • Entrepreneurship<br>• Problem Solving<br>• Technical Credibility |
| Business Acumen | • Financial Management<br>• Human Resources Management | • Technology Management |
| Building Coalitions/Communication | • Influencing/Negotiating<br>• Interpersonal Skills<br>• Oral Communication | • Partnering<br>• Political Savvy<br>• Written Communication |

*Source*:  OECD.

top civil servants, include ethics, wide-ranging government experience and knowledge, the ability to work in a team, developmental potential and proven interpersonal, communication and language skills.

## To identify and select potential leaders

Given the competence framework for future leaders, the next step is often to identify and select potential future leaders. This issue involves the choice of whether to select future leaders from outside or to nurture them within the public sector. If a country puts more emphasis on the former method rather than the latter, it should also address the question of how to recruit "the best and the brightest" candidates in competing with other sectors. In many OECD Member countries, the government faces difficulties in recruiting the most talented people to the public sector due to the worsening image of the government, tighter labour market, relatively low wage, and lack of entrepreneurship. For these countries, identifying and selecting future leaders has become more important than ever.

When looking at the OECD country case studies, there appear to be two broad trends in identifying and selecting leaders, although countries have not used the term of "leadership" explicitly. One group of countries like the UK, France, Japan, and Korea has a centralised system of selecting future managers and/or leaders. For example, the UK Government's fast stream process aims to select a pool of future leaders at an early stage. The ENA in France nurtures future elites of the whole society. In Japan and Korea, there is a special exam to recruit future managers and/or leaders. In contrast, countries like Sweden, Germany and the Netherlands, where personnel authorities were already largely devolved to the line ministries, do not have a formal government-wide system for selecting future managers/leaders. Rather, in these countries each ministry looks for the best-qualified person who fits its organisational needs.

Another way to identify leaders within the organisation is *succession planning*, which also plays an important role in heightening the morale of current employees. For those who are likely to be able to take leadership roles in the future, the organisation should provide a range of experiences in different functions, in various sectors, in inter-departmental task forces, and even in the private sector. Various experiences and involvement will help in developing future leaders in the organisation.

### To encourage mentoring and training

Once potential leaders are identified and selected, the next step is to continuously train them. As mentioned elsewhere, for this purpose, some countries set up a specialised institution for leadership development. For instance, the US Government established the Federal Executive Institutes and Management Development Centres, where public service leaders have a developmental pathway to leadership, known as the "Leadership Journey". In Sweden, the government set up the National Council for Quality and Development in 1999. One of the key tasks of this new institution is to recruit and train managers in public administration. For this purpose, it has conducted the "Strategic Management Programme", where the task of leadership, future trends, and activity development are covered.

Others, for instance Austria, Belgium, Finland, Japan, Korea, the Netherlands, Poland and Portugal, put greater emphasis on leadership in existing curricula and establish new training courses for the top executives or senior managers. For instance, Germany developed a four-phase system of leadership training in the Federal Academy of Public Administration as follows:

- Phase 1: competence training for future managers.
- Phase 2: qualification for leadership tasks.
- Phase 3: development of advanced leadership skills.
- Phase 4: special knowledge and exchange of experience.

The Netherlands has adopted, and Iceland plans, to adopt the "coaching and counselling" methods for present or potential leaders, in co-operation with private sector professionals. Under this method, for a certain period of time, a leader will discuss his/her weak points with the coach, and get advice from the coach for developing leadership competencies for the future. Iceland has taken an interesting approach to leadership development, whereby the government helps leaders to organise and maintain networks among themselves. This approach has been very useful for sharing common values among leaders as well as for learning from each other.

## To keep leadership development sustainable

As developing future leaders takes a long time, it is very important to keep the leadership development sustainable. To do so, some practical suggestions were raised at the OECD Symposium.

- Developing a comprehensive programme from the whole-of-government perspective is essential for developing future leaders. If possible, the government should set up some kind of institute specialised in leadership development.

- Allocating more of managers' time on developing leaders is crucial to the success of leadership development programmes. Research has revealed that one of the best practices in the most successful private businesses is for senior executives to spend up to 25% of their time developing leaders.

- Linking incentives with performance for better leadership encourages employees to sharpen their competencies and achieve their full potential. It also contributes to the organisation's sustained efforts to develop leaders.

Another way for the sustainable leadership development would be to create a group, such as Senior Civil Service Group. The US government has had scheme called Senior Executive Service (SES), while the UK has called it Senior Civil Service (SCS). The Netherlands introduced the Senior Public Service (SPS) system in 1995, and plans to enlarge the SPS gradually to all management positions in the national public service. The major advantage of this system is to integrate a loose collection of civil servants into a team of senior leaders sharing common values and visions for the future government. It helps not only to enhance the integrity of the civil service, but also to accelerate the mobility and flexibility among top leaders in the public sector.

## 5. Further issues

## Women leaders in the public sector

As the concern about gender equality grows in OECD Member countries, the issue of women leaders in the civil service seems to be one of the most unexplored, but an important area in leadership development. According to the

27

survey, very few countries mentioned the issue of women leaders in the civil service. Norway addressed this issue by setting up a four-year plan to increase the number of women in top and middle managers from 22% in 1997 to 30% in 2001.

In general, over the last decade, it appears that there has been a significant increase in the number of women in the civil service. In particular, women are more heavily represented in the public sector than in the economy as a whole in many OECD Member countries. Despite the increasing proportion of women in the civil service, it appears that the number of women in managerial and senior level posts is still relatively low. In most countries represented in Figure 3, the proportion of women in their respective top occupational group post is shown to be about 20% or less, with the exception of France.[4]

However, during the last decade, the number of women managers increased drastically in some countries and moderately in other countries. As can be seen in Figure 3, during the 1990s the UK has seen about a 125% increase in the number of woman managers. It can be explained in part by the fact that steps have been taken to promote equal employment opportunities between men and women in some countries. It is also expected that the proportion of women leaders in the civil service will increase in the future thanks to the equal employment policies which are widespread in OECD Member countries.

Figure 3.    **Change in the civil service leaders: women and total**

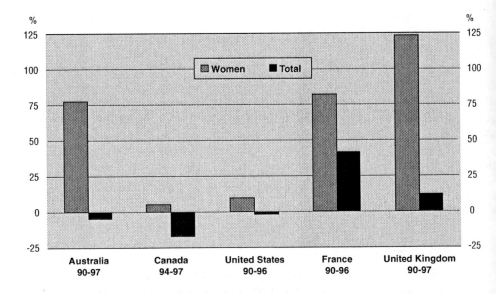

*Source:* OECD.

## Securing balances

Developing an elite leadership cadre has many advantages. It promotes common values and vision among public sector leaders. Also it helps to enhance policy coherence among departments. Furthermore, it contributes to widening perspectives of leaders, by providing opportunities for different knowledge and experience. However there are some possible dangers in developing leadership in this way. If a group of leaders begins to pursue their own interests rather than its national interest, the country may suffer. Such a group may become closed and insufficiently responsive to wide changes in society. So new problems on the agenda are how to build a leadership cadre that is more responsive or representative, and also, how to re-orient and refresh existing cadres if they have begun to get out of step with the society they represent.

An interesting question is how to manage an elite system in circumstances where public management requires more leadership at all levels. Clearly the danger to avoid is that of empowering a minority at the expense of the motivation of the majority.

## Different problems need different solutions

Many Member countries are looking to the strengthening of leadership as the solution to national public challenges. How they approach leadership however needs to be in reference to the kinds of problems being faced. It seems important for leadership strategies to be based on a clear diagnosis of the national challenges being faced, and the current characteristics of the public sector culture – pursuing "leadership" development without that diagnosis and strategy is likely to be ineffective. If a public service is excessively clannish, for instance, the leadership development strategy might give more attention to diversity and innovation, while a public service with problems of atomisation might be looking to strengthen collective values. A rule-bound public service might look for more citizen focus, while a poorly compliant public service might aim for leaders able to apply stronger behavioural controls.

## Leadership development policy implications

From experience and analysis to date certain lessons about how to approach the task of leadership development suggest themselves:

- A public sector leadership course would have an agenda somewhat different from a normal leadership development course. Any intervention focused on public sector leadership should deal less with systems and skills but have at its heart the actual public sector challenges confronting the group in question and the public sector values and personal values that those challenges threaten.

- The best way to become a leader is by doing it or by working closely with people who do it. If we find we cannot look at leadership as a set of individual competencies separate from one's own willingness to face tough issues, then leadership is learnt by facing tough issues and by working with people who make you face tough issues.

- Leadership development should not be confined to those who hold positions of high authority. Emergent senior managers surely warrant special attention, but a leadership development strategy confined to that group ignores the fact that influence is more informal than formal and that successful adaptation requires personal responsibility at all levels.

- Successful leadership requires not only focusing on the issues but a deep understanding of the people involved and how they react to stress. It also requires a clear sense of what problems are most important and how many can be dealt with at one time, as well as a capacity to dampen down conflict and create an environment in which people have the security and confidence to face up to issues rather than avoiding them or being overwhelmed by them.

- Finally, it also requires a robust sense of what people might do, and in what sequence, to begin changing their circumstances.

Government efforts to stimulate leadership in the sense of the knowledge, skills and moral courage necessary for effective, adaptive public sector action, should be less a technical or knowledge transfer than a whole-hearted effort at facing hard issues, promoting values and stimulating robust action. Deeply involved in any such process should be those who are already demonstrating effective leadership.

### Areas for future attention

Any successful leadership strategy involves culture change. We know that both culture change is very difficult, and that where it does take place it is over a long period and in response to a variety of powerful pressures. In strengthening OECD efforts in this area, it is clear that we need better quality information on the degree to which past public sector leadership promotion strategies have actually changed behaviour. On this basis, countries will be better placed to diagnose the current problem and formulate strategies which are likely to be effective. There is scope for research and exchanges on comparative national expectations of leadership, cadre models, diversity goals and tools, feeder strategies, gender emphasis, nature and duration of acculturalisation strategies, degrees of central direction and control, and how to assess the relative impact of nurturing, training and buying strategies and the mixtures thereof.

## Notes

1. Jo Brosnahan, 1999, "Public Sector Reform Requires Leadership", A paper presented to the OECD/PUMA Symposium on Government of the Future in September 1999.
2. See Ronald A. Heifetz, 1994, *Leadership Without Easy Answers*.
3. See OECD, 2000, *Government of the Future*.
4. See OECD [PUMA/HRM(2000)7], *The PSPE (Public Sector Pay and Employment) Update and Future HRM Data Collection*, document presented to the HRM Working Party Meeting in July 2000.

© OECD 2001

Chapter 2

# Leadership Development Strategies in the UK Civil Service*

## 1. Introduction

This paper describes recent and continuing work to modernise the approach to leadership development in the UK Civil Service. This work is in the context of a major programme to reform the Civil Service and to make it fit for the 21st century. This programme is itself a response to the publication of the Modernising Government White Paper in March 1999.

The Civil Service reform programme is in its early stages and is seen as a long-term programme of change taking three to five years. This paper will describe work underway centrally, led by the Cabinet Office, to ensure we have the leaders the Civil Service needs for the future. Whilst it is too early to be sure what impact these initiatives will have, a number of key issues concerning change management and leadership development strategies have already been identified which should be of interest to other public service organisations interested in enhancing their leadership capability.

### The UK civil service

The size, structure and management of the UK Civil Service have changed significantly over the last 15 years. The Civil Service currently employs around 475 000 people, making up about 2% of the UK workforce and about 10% of the public sector as a whole. The majority of civil servants are engaged in providing services to the general public such as helping them find jobs, paying social security benefits and issuing driving licences. Others provide advice and information to ministers and develop policy. Civil servants in the service delivery areas are employed in executive agencies whilst policy issues are dealt with by central departments. At 1 April 1999 there were 111 agencies or organisations operating on agency lines, employing nearly 80% of civil servants.

---

\* This paper was prepared and presented to the OECD HRM meeting in July 2000 by Mr. Malcolm Dawson, Head of SCS Performance Management and Pay, Cabinet Office.

Since April 1996, all departments and agencies have had delegated responsibility for the pay and grading of their staff, except for those in the Senior Civil Service (SCS). The SCS consists of the top 3 000 civil servants across all departments and agencies. They have a common pay and grading system distinct from that in their employing department or agency and there is an element of central career management and training and development provision. Departments and agencies are, however, responsible for the day-to-day management of all their staff both at and below the SCS and for most individual HRM decisions.

The creation of executive agencies and the delegation of pay and grading are examples of the changes in the 1980s and 1990s aimed at creating a more managerial, efficient and customer-focused organisation. Performance-related pay has been in use throughout the Civil Service since the early 1990s. Almost all departments and agencies are now recognised as Investors in People – the national standard for effective training and development. The European Foundation for Quality Management Excellence Model is used by more than two-thirds of agencies. Key targets for all departments are published in Public Service Agreements and supported by internal business planning processes. In short, there has been an enormous change in the nature of the Civil Service over the last two decades. Yet, it is clear that we need to do much more.

### Civil service reform

The Modernising Government White Paper published in March 1999 set out a long-term programme of change for all UK public services. It had three aims: to ensure that policy is more joined-up and strategic *i.e.* that it is more forward looking and better integrates the activities of different organisations; to make sure that public services are focused on the needs of users, not organised around the convenience of providers; and to ensure we deliver public services which are of high quality and efficient. It committed public services to being more responsive to people's needs, to being more inclusive and fair and to harnessing new technology to meet the needs of citizens and businesses. It was clear from the White Paper that the culture of public service organisations had to change and that public servants needed to develop new skills and attitudes. The White Paper included a specific commitment that the Civil Service would put in train a programme to modernise itself and that a report on progress would be published later in the year.

The Civil Service Reform Report from the Head of the Civil Service, Sir Richard Wilson, to the Prime Minister was published in December 1999[1] for details of the main report, supporting sub-group reports and the first annual report on progress). It set out an ambitious programme to "create a more open, diverse and professional Civil Service" whilst building on the enduring core values of integrity, propriety, political impartiality and selection on merit. It is based around six key themes:

34

- stronger leadership with a clear sense of purpose;

- better business planning;
- sharper performance management;
- a dramatic improvement in diversity;
- a service more open to people and ideas, which brings on talent;
- better conditions for staff.

## 2. Importance of leadership

The report recognised that leadership – both corporate and individual – is crucial to achieving change. It called for transformational leaders throughout departments and agencies who set an example of the kind of behaviour required, work corporately and across institutional boundaries to deliver the outcomes the government is seeking, and who are able to articulate and gain commitment to a vision of the direction in which their organisation is heading. The Civil Service needs better leaders at all levels, but it particularly needs them at the top. If change does not happen at the top, it will not happen at all.

## 3. Leadership development strategy

The strategy for enhancing our leadership capability described in the Civil Service Reform Report has three elements.

### Defining what sort of leadership we want now and in the future and making appointments on that basis

In evaluating the effectiveness of our leadership development activities it became obvious that a major issue was whether we were clear about what we were trying to achieve through such interventions and what sort of leaders we want. It was an issue which was repeatedly raised in the course of developing the reform programme. The Cabinet Office is leading two projects intended to help better define what leadership we want and what sort of leaders we should be developing. These two projects – developing a new competence framework for the Senior Civil Service and defining leadership attributes and measures – are described in more detail below.

### Establishing better targeted and more effective development programmes

There is strong evidence that we are not good enough at spotting internal talent and then making the most of it. The Civil Service is also finding it increasingly difficult to attract the best people – whether graduates or mid-career – into the service. We are putting in place a range of initiatives intended to enhance our ability to identify talent at all levels and nurture these people by equipping them

35

with the range of skills and experience they will need in the modern Civil Service. Some examples of the work in hand include:

- Setting up mechanisms for talent spotting within departments. This includes agreeing on a model approach which might be adapted by departments and drawing up best practice guidance.

- The Civil Service is also establishing a new Public Service Leaders Scheme to train a cohort of our best internal talent alongside managers from the wider public sector. The scheme would ensure that Civil Service participants gain experience in other public sector organisations. The aim is to contribute to the improved delivery of public services by developing a pool of future leaders with enhanced capacity to work in partnership with other public sector organisations. The scheme will achieve this by giving public servants with high potential experience in different parts of the public sector to enhance their knowledge and understanding of linked activities and to expose them to new situations, challenges and thinking.

- Departments are reviewing and revising their internal development programmes to ensure they are better focused on enhancing our leadership capability at all levels.

- Finally, all senior civil servants will have undertaken 360 degree feedback by the end of 2001 which will be linked to personal development programmes. It is widely accepted that a key element in effective leadership is self-awareness and an understanding of the impact of the leader's behaviour on others. The 360 degree programme is intended to ensure that all senior civil servants have an opportunity to find out how their peers, subordinates and in some cases external contacts, as well as their line managers, view them. The assessment is for developmental purposes only and does not contribute to the annual performance review process. The feedback gathered is confidential to the individual and does not have to be shared with line managers. Assessment is primarily against the SCS competences – a revised 360 degree questionnaire will be developed to match the new SCS competences once they are finalised.

### Creating a more open and diverse Civil Service

The Civil Service is acknowledged to be too insular, not reflecting the diversity of modern society. We need to improve our ability to attract and develop the best from all sections of society, dispel outdated stereotypes of civil servants, attract more people at mid-career and ensure that the SCS is more outward-looking and has broader experience. Key actions to achieve this include:

- Redefining the fast stream (the graduate recruitment scheme for high flyers) to broaden entry, clarify exactly what we are looking for in our graduate-calibre recruits, and re-design the selection process accordingly.

- Over the next 10 years achieve a 10% year-on-year increase in open competitions for middle and senior managers. This will be aimed particularly at bringing in new thinking and skills which are in short supply in the Civil Service such as project management, e-commerce skills and leadership of service delivery organisations.

- Increase the level of interchange between the Civil Service and other sectors of the economy with the aim that, by 2005, 65% of the SCS will have had experience outside the Civil Service.

- Using Internet technology to provide better access to information about jobs in the Civil Service. A Website has been set up on the Government Secure Intranet to advertise internal vacancies in the Civil Service and a parallel site has been set up on the Internet to advertise open competition vacancies and provide information about how to join the Civil Service.

- Working to change the image of the Civil Service portrayed in the media and through recruitment advertising. Supporting this by employing outreach workers and specialist advisers to help change attitudes to the organisation amongst minority ethnic and other groups.

## 4. Examples of efforts towards defining leadership

The UK Civil Service has two projects underway aimed at defining the leadership we need.

### SCS *competences*

In the first Cabinet Office project, as part of a wider project to reform the pay and performance management systems for the Senior Civil Service, we have developed a new SCS core competence framework. The framework replaces one which has been in place since the creation of the Senior Civil Service in 1996. The aim was to develop a framework which better reflects the more diverse, creative, strategic and people-centred organisation we need to become. The first draft of the framework was produced at the beginning of April 2000. It was developed on the basis of evidence gathered in interviews with key stakeholders (the Head of the Civil Service, Heads of Departments, Personnel Directors, external partners etc.); workshops with people below the SCS to see what they were looking for from their leaders; critical incident interviews with a cross-section of high performing senior civil servants; and benchmark research into current practice in the public and private sectors both in the UK and internationally.

The draft of the new framework was significantly different in a number of ways. The presentation was simpler and more user-friendly. It was entirely behaviourally based, the aim being both to make it easier to use and to signal much more

37

clearly that what leaders do has much greater impact than what they say. The framework also focused more tightly on a smaller number of competences which really make a difference to the performance of senior civil servants. A final innovation in the draft framework was the inclusion of descriptions of both effective and ineffective behaviours to assist with analysing performance and discussing development needs. The frame workplaces leadership at the heart of the framework as the key element that reflects the unique contribution we expect from the SCS. It does this not by having a specific competence or competences for leadership, but by reflecting leadership behaviours in *every* competence in the framework.

The draft competence framework was approved by the Civil Service Management Board in May 2000 as the basis for an extensive consultation, validation and pilot testing exercise. The validation and piloting programme was intended to test both the content of the framework and its practical application in the various processes for which it is designed. The validation process was based upon a survey of all members of the SCS and workshops with groups of both SCS and non-SCS civil servants. We ran 10 workshops to test the content of the framework with people both in and below the SCS. The paper survey asked SCS members to fill in a questionnaire about what they thought of the framework and also offered them the opportunity to go to the Cabinet Office web site to fill in an on-line self assessment against the new competences and then give feedback about the process. This additional self-assessment element also contributed to an analysis of the possible training implications of the new framework.

The pilot programme was run in partnership with 14 departments and agencies. They tested the use of the competences in a range of applications including 360 degree feedback, self-assessment, development centres, training courses, coaching and shadow appraisals.

In approving progress to the second stage, the Civil Service Management Board had expressed particular concerns about whether the framework promoted diversity sufficiently. To address this issue, 3 of the 10 workshops focused specifically on people from under-represented groups (women, ethnic minorities and disabled people) to establish whether the draft framework adequately reflected their concerns. In parallel with the testing we also consulted the Equal Opportunities Commission, Commission for Racial Equality and Disability Rights Commission as well independent experts in the field.

The validation and pilots along with the additional research into diversity were complete by September 2000. By the end of the two stages around 900 people had contributed to the development of the framework. The results revealed strong support for the general approach adopted, whilst identifying a number of areas where the framework could be improved. The language was further simplified and sharpened; a greater focus on the delivery of results was introduced; two of the six competences were significantly re-structured; and behaviours which promote diversity were made more explicit. A revised framework with an updated presentation was approved by the Civil Service Management Board in November.[2] It has been widely welcomed as a significant improvement over the existing criteria and a potentially powerful catalyst for change and enhanced leadership capacity. The framework was integrated into the new SCS pay and performance management system in April 2001 and will provide an input to appointments, selection and development processes as well as pay decisions.

## New Civil Service leadership

The second project, linked to the work on SCS competences, is one intended to define in greater detail the attributes of effective Civil Service leaders; in other words, to define what leaders need to be, know and do. This New Civil Service Leadership project is initially focused on the SCS, particularly those in the top 600 posts, and is designed to give us a more three dimensional picture of the leader of the future than can be gained from competences alone. The project is in two stages and the outputs will be integrated into recruitment, selection and development processes for senior posts. In the first stage we conducted qualitative research aimed at mapping out the ground and getting a broad picture from people both within and outside the Civil Service of what sort of leaders we need and what sort of challenges they face. A number of key issues emerged from the interviews with civil servants, particularly those at the top:

- Leaders versus leadership – the mind-set of civil servants was that leadership was a function of role *i.e.* head of unit, head of division, head of department, and that this brought with it certain responsibilities and demands. The idea of leadership as a way of behaving which anyone could demonstrate *i.e.* as a team member was not one to which they immediately related.

- Civil servants are good at managing upwards *i.e.* managing senior managers and ministers, but poor at managing down within their teams, outwards to partner organisations and stakeholders and across their organisation.

- There was some nervousness about the concept of transformational leadership – is this something which is appropriate in a public service organisation where stability and reliability are also important?

- Will more leadership necessarily be better and result in better outcomes?

- There was a strong feeling that leadership in the public sector was inherently more difficult due to the complexity and ambiguity of the circumstances in which civil servants have to operate. Any new definition of leadership has to reflect that dimension, but some felt that the sheer difficulty of demonstrating what they defined as leadership meant that trying to promote more was a fruitless exercise.

39

- Most of the people interviewed carried with them their own definition of what leadership is. Often this revolved around some of the traditional heroic and charismatic models associated with the military or entrepreneurs. This model was seen as inappropriate in a central government organisation in which the relationship between civil servants and ministers and Parliamentary accountability has a significant impact on behaviour. This dimension to public sector leadership was reflected in a number of references to the importance of values and ethics. Respondents were clear that an important element of leadership in the Civil Service is demonstrating both organisational and personal values.

- We do not want clones. It is important that we recognise that there is a range of styles of leadership which will be appropriate and effective in different situations. The new definition must recognise and value these differences. Equally, there are clearly styles and approaches we do not want.

During this initial phase of research we were able to establish parameters for the leadership we need based on a combination of the views of current and future leaders and the reform agenda. We have also been able to establish some principles about the nature of leadership which will guide further work. These are that leadership:

- is essentially future focused, concerned with making the future better than the past;

- can be learned and developed – some leaders are born, but the majority are made;

- takes many forms – there is no one best way, but although challenges vary and approaches differ the underlying qualities and processes are essentially the same;

- in a devolved organisation structure where decisions are increasingly taken at the front line, it is clear that leadership is needed at all levels, not just the top;

- is fundamentally about building effective relationships;

- is concerned with turning inputs, whether individual, team or organisational, into results.

The parameters for our definition of New Civil Service Leadership are that leadership entails:

- focus on delivery of results;

- challenging assumptions;

- being open to learning from outside;

- understanding the environment and its impact;

- thinking and acting strategically;
- building new patterns and ways of working;
- developing and communicating a personal vision of change.

## 5. Future programme

This provides us with the skeleton which we now need to flesh out. We are about to commence Stage 2 of the leadership attributes project during which we aim to identify the specific attributes which will enable our leaders to deliver this challenging agenda. The plan is to invite a sample of civil servants, including current high performing senior civil servants, people on the verge of promotion to the SCS and people on development programmes, to a series of leadership challenge workshops. They will undertake a selection of psychometric assessments and take part in a selection of case study simulations intended to test what leadership choices they make in differing situations. The aim is to develop descriptors of the attributes of successful Civil Service leaders as defined by their personal characteristics, competences, professional skills and experience. This will include an analysis of the differences, if any, between the requirements of Civil Service and non-Civil Service leadership. The process of identifying the attributes will also enable us to establish what combination of psychometric tools might best serve as tests of leadership potential.

### Expected outcomes and lessons

Our work to develop a clearer picture of the leadership we need will provide an important contribution to ensuring that our leadership development activities are effectively targeted and focused. However, the outputs in terms of the competence framework, the description of the form of New Civil Service leadership and the norms and measures to help identify potential and make appointments are only a step on the way. Taken together, the leadership development strategy we are now pursuing is intended to achieve five strategic objectives which are set out in the Bringing in and Bringing on Talent Civil Service Reform Report.

- provide the individuals for strategic leadership of the service with the relevant experience;
- create a broader based, more professional Senior Civil Service with outside experience;
- spot and develop talent;
- recruit in mid-career;
- create a broader, more diverse base across the whole of the Civil Service.

41

The process of taking forward this range of initiatives, and particularly the work to define the new form of Civil Service leadership, however, has raised a number of issues.

There are tensions inherent in a decentralised organisation in trying to balance a) the flexibility needed to reflect the diversity of roles and situations of Civil Service leaders with b) the need for a framework which is simple and understandable and with c) producing something which has real utility. The ever-present danger is that outcome is one which fails on all three criteria. It became clear early on that it would be important to integrate and capitalise on current activity across the Civil Service – we are not working on a blank canvas and failing to recognise this runs the risk of alienating key stakeholders, some of whom will inevitably have conflicting interests.

An issue which the initial research unearthed was the difficulty of developing a description of successful leadership for the future whilst drawing on the views and analysis of performance of a crop of our current and potential leaders. A perennial problem is trying to gaze into the crystal ball and predict what future demands there will be on an organisation. In terms of change management, we were presented with the need to strike the right balance between moving the leadership agenda forward and changing attitudes, whilst at the same time not moving so far that the outputs are dismissed as not being viable. The key to this and many other aspects of making real progress was the importance of finding and using champions who support the programme and are in a position to influence others. Finally – and perhaps paradoxically – we have recognised that we need leadership now, particularly from the top, if we are to be successful in implementing our strategy for developing the leaders of the future. This reflects a key responsibility of senior leaders as stewards for whom a high priority should be not just the short term success but the long term health of the organisation.

## Notes

1. See www.cabinet-office.gov.uk/civilservice-reform/index.htm.
2. See the new competence framework and final report at www.cabinet-office.gov.uk/civilservice/scscompetencies/index.htm.

# Chapter 3

# Leadership Development in the United States*

## 1. Introduction

The US Office of Personnel Management (OPM) is committed to developing leadership talent to serve America in the 21st century. If we are to provide the type of services expected by our customers – the American people – we believe a special type of leader is required. Further, we recognise that today's world economy and global marketplace also dictates that this new enlightened world class public executive/leader possess different skills than was necessary in the past. Historically, public service leaders required the traditional skills of leadership represented by the military model and rugged individualism. These traditional leaders were supported by legions of followers, had near total control, and directed their followers to their ultimate goal. In contrast, successful public service leaders today must work with their followers to solve problems rather than dictating solutions from the top of the hierarchy.

## 2. Why leadership is important

Leadership today requires a different approach to that of previous eras for at least three reasons:

- First, increasingly complex and interdependent public policy issues require innovative solutions. Creativity requires calling for the best ideas from everyone. The leader cannot solve the problems alone.
- Second, just having a creative solution does not mean you can implement it. Under the old autocratic model, leaders could expect to solve the problem, announce the decision, and get compliance, based on their authority. But public sector leaders today must gain commitment, not just compliance, and therefore a collaborative style is needed. Leaders now succeed only if they can influence others, and quite often those whose support they need do not report to them.

* This paper was prepared and presented to the OECD HRM meeting in July 2000 by Dr. Barbara Garvin-Kester, Director, Office of Executive and Management Development, Office of Personnel Management.

43

- Third, public sector leaders today cannot even expect those who report to them to follow orders – nor should they. Today's followers have many choices. Given an unemployment rate in the US of less than 4% – the lowest it has been since 1970 – our labour market requires a level of competitiveness that we have not seen in a generation. American workers, especially the youngest, thrive on challenges and controlling their work environment. Without professional stimulation and the ability to exercise leadership, they pick up their portable pensions, portable skills and portable computers and sell their talents to another labour market bidder. From a purely economic viewpoint the retention of highly skilled practitioners is a critical matter for public service leaders. Leadership skills that energise followers are obviously essential.

But public leaders face an even greater challenge than gaining followers through effective leadership skills. They must accomplish this while operating within the guidelines of our Constitution. They must promote democracy at the same time as they accomplish programme goals. To succeed programmatically while damaging the fabric of democracy is to fail. This is why, at its core, public service leadership and leadership development must be based upon values. The democratic leader differs from the demagogue in the values represented. Where those values are moral and call for the best in others, they build democracy. When they are immoral, they lead to rule by force or arms, not ideals. Thus, leadership based on core values anchored in our Constitution is especially critical for America's public service leaders. The Constitution demands that we seek to provide skilled leadership. Our political leaders exhort us to help develop extraordinary leaders and, perhaps as important as anything else, the public holds the government executive accountable to conduct the nation's business in a responsible manner.

Given our belief and acceptance that effective leadership is both necessary and valued, OPM recognises that strategies for continuous investment in learning and development are critical to ensuring improved government performance and the success of our public sector leaders.

## 3. Strategies to build and enhance leadership skills

The US Office of Personnel Management (OPM)'s goal for building and enhancing the leadership skills of our senior Civil Service is to transform our government training and development to focus on performance improvement with results that support agency missions and goals. One strategy to accomplish this has been to define a set of key characteristics and leadership competencies, called Executive Core Qualifications (ECQs), which are used for the selection of new members to the Senior Executive Service (SES) – the most senior public

44

service leaders. OPM has defined and validated these competencies through an ongoing programme of research conducted by our own psychologists in co-operation with leading experts in the assessment field. This research dates back well over twenty years and has seen the evolution of our models of leadership from those suitable for a traditional, hierarchical bureaucracy to an approach that can better serve the reinvented government of the 21st century. There are five ECQs made up of 27 competencies (a complete list of competencies is given in Appendix). These five ECQs are:

- **Leading Change,** which encourages creative thinking while it integrates national and programme goals and priorities to improve customer service and programme performance.

- **Leading People,** which focuses on maximising employee potential and fostering high ethical standards.

- **Results Driven,** stressing results through accountability and continuous improvement.

- **Business Acumen,** which focuses on the use of new technology and information resources to improve decision making.

- **Building Coalitions and Communications**, emphasising the ability to explain, advocate and express ideas in a convincing way, the ability to negotiate with individuals and groups, and the ability to develop an expansive, professional network.

These ECQs are used to:

- identify developmental needs of individuals in formal OPM-approved candidate development programmes;

- select and certify candidates for the Senior Executive Service (SES);

- measure performance in the first year of service of these newly appointed leaders.

The ECQs also form the basis for our executive and management development curriculum. Our Office of Executive and Management Development (OEMD) provides inter-agency, residential leadership training and development at the Federal Executive Institute (FEI) in Charlottesville, Virginia, and our Management Development Centers in Shepherdstown, West Virginia, and Aurora, Colorado. Through OEMD, our public service leaders have a developmental pathway to leadership, known as the "Leadership Journey", which provides assessment programmes, training seminars, and continuous learning opportunities based upon the ECQs and taught within the values and framework of our Constitution.

45

*Leadership journey*

This offers our executives a pathway for development that follows them throughout their entire careers and supports them in career and succession planning. It comprises the following assessment programmes, continuous curriculum path, and follow-up experiences:

- One-week assessment programmes offered at both the Management Development Centers (MDCs) and the Federal Executive Institute (FEI). These are designed to help people identify their skill strengths and needs against the 27 ECQ competencies and develop plans to build their skills. Assessment is a critical approach to helping keep people on their career tracks and avoiding "derailment" at key career transition points.

- A Leadership Potential Seminar (LPS) which lays the foundation for an entire leadership career. It helps those who have not yet entered leadership identify what it will take to succeed as a leader and decide whether they wish to build leadership as a "second career". The design is based on research conducted by the Center for Creative Leadership in Greensboro, NC, as well as focus group feedback from our graduates.

- A Supervisory Leadership Seminar (SLS) emphasises those ECQ competencies that are needed by a newly selected supervisor, including such competencies as project management and basic administrative and human resource skills.

- Our Seminar for New Managers (SNM) is designed to help the new manager supervise and emphasises "Leading People".

- The Management Development Seminar (MDS) is a "tune up" for the experienced manager that focuses on organisational leadership skills.

- The Executive Development Seminar (EDS) is for the manager who is making the transition to the executive level and it addresses skills such as political savvy, understanding policy, developing external relationships and leading organisational change.

- Finally, the Leadership for a Democratic Society Program (LDS) at FEI expands on EDS and allows for a more tailored, in-depth experience in leading organisation change. It emphasises "Building Coalitions and Communication" skills.

Additional programmes offered by FEI's Center for Executive Leadership (CEL) and at our MDCs provide in-depth knowledge and skill practice for particular competencies, skill sets or subject matter. These additional programmes are not just "add-ons" for a successful executive. They are continual learning opportunities for current executives and developmental activities for future executives that are critical for delivering agency results expected by the

46

American people. CEL also provides on-site executive coaching and consulting that is often needed for continuous learning to ensure successful implementation of new skills/knowledge and to keep executives up-to-date in their skills even after Senior Executive Service (SES) certification.

## 4. Practical examples of leadership training

### *Leadership for a democratic society program*

The Leadership for a Democratic Society Program (LDS) is an excellent example of how values and skills development are integrated in an inter-agency, residential programme to provide a complete and holistic experience for our senior executives. Skills in the service of democratic values are at the core of this curriculum. Within the overarching framework of constitutional governance, the programme focuses on four curriculum themes.

- Personal leadership (curriculum theme 1) is at the core because leaders must understand themselves and how their values shape their assumptions, beliefs, and actions. They must also understand their strengths and how those strengths can be used to compensate for blind spots. They must be able to change themselves if they hope to change anything or anyone else. The entire first week is spent on enabling executives to know and begin to change themselves.
- Changing oneself, however, is not sufficient for improving government. Executives must also be able to transform their organisation (curriculum theme 2).
- They must do so within a policy framework that involves the Congress, the courts, the media, interest groups and others (curriculum theme 3).
- And, they must recognise and gain skills in working in the broader context that forms US society and the world outside our borders (curriculum theme 4).

These four themes are presented in the Leadership for a Democratic Society (LDS) Program through the following curriculum approaches:

### *Leadership proceeds from within*

Through self-assessments, instrumented feedback (including data from peers, direct reports, and superiors), and small-group sharing and feedback, each executive leaves the programme with three core questions:

- What got me to where I am?
- What is the next step I want to take?
- What do I need to take with me (and what do I need to leave behind) for the next step?

47

A Leadership Development Team – a small group of eight to nine executives aided by a faculty facilitator – helps each member explore these questions through group exercises and personal reflection.

### The leader is a whole person and leads whole people

Leaders and followers have physical needs as well as intellectual ones. They possess dreams as well as data. The LDS programme pays attention to the whole person, including physical wellness, emotional health, and personal financial fitness. A curriculum that cares about the whole person is more likely to produce whole executives who care about the whole employee. In addition to a computerised health risk appraisal and (optional) blood draw, the programme offers general sessions on such topics as nutrition, stress management and health issues at mid-life.

### Learning comes from expectation failure

No one ever learned by doing something flawlessly the first time. The programme provides an atmosphere that encourages people to stretch in a risk-free environment. Participants engage in case studies, simulations, and skill-based courses (with videotaped feedback).

### Everyone is a teacher and a learner

As much teaching takes place among executives as it does among executives and faculty. Executives teach about work-related experiences through an evening forum series and share their skills and best practices. Faculty continue to learn from their interactions with participants both in and out of the classroom.

### A residential setting fosters a corporate view

People solve problems by surmounting technical, organisational and jurisdictional barriers and by trusting other people on the other side of the issue. By sharing time informally, the executives begin to appreciate one another's "back home" issues and build the working relationships that broaden their view and lead them to help each other after graduation.

### Choice

Over the course of four weeks, each executive may choose three courses from the twelve offered with additional choices in plenary sessions, wellness activities, executive fora and independent study options using our library and faculty.

*Applied learning through leadership challenges*

The programme emphasis is on theory and concepts applied in real world settings. It concludes with the executive addressing four questions:

- What are my core values?
- What are the purposes of our organisation?
- What goals do we need to reach?
- What changes do I need to make in myself?

The executive is then asked to present these questions in a narrative statement to share with other participants in a compelling way. Participants lend counsel and encouragement to help shape the critical challenge the executive presents to his organisation or agency upon returning home.

The Leadership for a Democratic Society Program is our capstone program that strives to help leaders develop to the best of their potential. It shows them how to lead by example from a base of deeply held moral values, and how to challenge their would-be followers to solve the nation's problems.

### Treasury Executive Leadership Program

Another key strategy that is aimed at improving government performance is helping agencies integrate their human resource strategies, goals, and objectives into agency strategic plans. The Office of Executive and Management Development (OEMD) is engaged in establishing strategic partnerships with agencies to help them design learning and development initiatives that support their strategic direction and ensure success. Currently, the OEMD has developed strategic partnerships with twelve different agencies. One excellent example of how these partnerships help agencies better align their human resource initiatives with their strategic plans is found in the US Treasury Department.

In 1998, Treasury Secretary Robert Rubin called together all of his direct reports to discuss human resource issues. This was the first time in US Treasury history that this group of executives had been gathered to address such issues. During a wide-ranging discussion about the Department's leadership corps, participants realised that the Treasury Department did a good job preparing people for the executive ranks, but did little for the executives themselves. Treasury asked the Federal Executive Institute's (FEI's) Center for Executive Leadership (CEL) to work in partnership with them to develop an intense training programme. The main objectives were to create a programme that would enhance the Executive Core Qualifications and competencies most critical to success at Treasury, and to integrate opportunities for networking across the diverse bureaus within the Department.

49

Following several collaborative design meetings, FEI developed a two-week "split" residential programme, the Treasury Executive Leadership Program. During the first week, executives learn about their personal effectiveness through assessments, exploration of the science of leadership and the art of gaining followers, effective leadership communication, managing change, and executive coaching skills. At the end of the first week, each executive sets personal action goals. They return three months later to discuss experiences around their action plans and to focus on organisational effectiveness. Each cohort of 16-20 executives (of which there have been eight over the past year and a half) has an "Executive Sponsor" selected from Treasury's most senior ranks to act as a catalyst both in the classroom and back on the job. The programme is developing a wide base of support in the Department as Senior Executive Service (SES) members return to work with enthusiastic reviews. An extensive critical incident interview process is in progress to learn more about what participants have put into practice and how the programme can continue to meet its objectives.

An important by-product of the Treasury Executive Leadership Program has been the creation of a community of learning and leadership that appears to last beyond the classroom. Participants view themselves as a core leadership resource for the Department and are preparing to pilot a new FEI development programme based on Action Learning principles that will enable them to continue to deepen their leadership skills while addressing specific strategic business issues.

### Other strategies for building and enhancing skills

OPM wants to foster more learning opportunities where executives meet and interact with other executives. OPM's Office of Executive Resource Management (OERM) and Office of Executive and Management Development (OEMD) are working together to offer more leadership symposiums and other fora for exchanging ideas and networking. Towards this effort, OPM is partnering with agencies to provide an electronic clearinghouse for such opportunities. Surveys with our SES members indicate that job "mobility" may improve performance. In response, OPM is undertaking initiatives to broaden the viewpoints and experiences of our executives by providing them with development opportunities in various agencies and by seeking government-wide authority for private sector exchanges that would expose SES members to best practices.

Technology is also a key strategy that is revolutionising the way our leaders learn. Under OPM leadership, more than 31 federal agencies are working on projects that illustrate different applications of learning technology in a Federal environment. The Department of Labor is delivering employment law training to Federal employees by using "expert systems", *i.e.*, software programmes that allow employees to ask questions and receive immediate guidance on legal issues and tactics. Training for emergency response teams is being delivered by the Department of Defence with networked PCs coupled with sophisticated 3-D virtual simulations. The Department of State is teaching sixty foreign languages using a hybrid approach – coupling computer-based training with satellite down-links and the Internet. For our executives, our Center for Executive Leadership (CEL) provides a week-long course that simulates a virtual working environment and teaches leaders and their team how to manage effectively in these new workplaces. The OEMD is also constructing a "technology backbone" that will allow executives and managers to register for development programmes on-line, complete their pre-programme materials and assessments on-line, submit evaluations electronically, access and learn about best practices, and engage in web-based simulations for continuous learning.

### Measures of success

In 1979, our government reorganised its senior leadership structure by creating the Senior Executive Service (SES). There are currently 6 778 members, 5 991 of whom are career civil servants while the remainder are appointed by the President and change with each administration. Career members must be certified by an independent Qualifications Review Board (QRB) based on the ECQs established by the OPM. As previously stated, these same ECQs are used to develop a pool of applicants ready to enter the SES through participation in Candidate Development Programs. The Leadership Journey Programme developed by the OEMD provides the training and experiences that executives and managers need to meet these qualifications and pass the QRB. If unsuccessful, candidates are required to identify and improve the areas in which they are deficient.

The OEMD evaluates the effectiveness of its Leadership Journey curriculum at several different levels. Using the Kirkpatrick model of evaluation, we assess participant acceptance and appropriateness of the design and delivery of our programmes (Level 1 evaluation). OEMD programmes consistently score above 4.5 on a 5-point scale. We also use case studies, role play, and our Leadership Challenges Programme to measure student learning within the classroom (Level 2 evaluation). We conduct follow-up studies with graduate executives to monitor the application of these changes on the job (Level 3 evaluation). And, we are instituting a return on investment programme to assess the impact of our programmes on the federal government. For example, last year we collected data on our Virtual Collaboration Workshop which revealed that our participants had met their short-term action plan goals to improve agency performance. Additional measures are currently being used to assess improved agency performance.

The following is a table from one of our evaluation studies at the Federal Executive Institute. Two executives in our Leadership for a Democratic Society (LDS) Program were interviewed to assess more fully return on investment.

51

| Agency | Application of Knowledge – Level 3 | Organisation Results – Level 4 |
|---|---|---|
| Executive #1 Interior | 1. Designed 25-item instrument to further test improvement in areas of benchmarks with low scores.<br>2. Acknowledged staff's conflict of interest and fired children of staff. | Statistically significant improvements in areas of:<br>1. Straightforwardness and Composure (reduced cynicism, hostility, moodiness, and blaming of others).<br>2. Quick Study (mastering new knowledge and skills). |
| Executive #2 EPA | 1. Met with executive team to clarify expectations for work in his programme area.<br>2. Met with 4 Team Leaders to identify expectations for teams.<br>3. Created written document outlining expectations for team leaders.<br>4. Requested feedback and currently revising this document to everyone's satisfaction.<br>5. In his position, greater focus on simplifying problems and connecting people to other staff members with the answers. | 1. Re-energised one team leader. Previously, 70-75% chance she would leave her position. After this process, much less of a chance of attrition (20%).<br>2. One person decided to accept formal leadership for a team.<br>3. One team leader acknowledged greater scope of job responsibility than before.<br>4. Two more team leaders (four total) accepted responsibility for their budget.<br>5. More time for him to devote to projects for which he would not previously have had much time. |

*Source:*  OECD.

OEMD also aims to complete a total of six studies on the Kirkpatrick model to analyse further the impact leadership training has on individual executive and agency performance.

## 5.   Future development

We are pleased with the progress we have made, and have received positive affirmations from our customers. But no one can afford to become complacent. We recognise there are many issues in which we must remain constantly aware and willing to reinvent ourselves. Some of the most important of these are:

### Succession planning

The ageing of our government's leadership corps means that, in most federal agencies, half or more of the members of the SES will be eligible for voluntary retirement in the next few years. The departure of this leadership talent will leave agencies struggling to perform effectively unless they have prepared the next generation of leaders. By continuing to build strategic partnerships with agencies, we have an avenue to help them design and deliver succession planning programmes.

## Managing diversity

Government executives operate in a diverse world and an increasingly diverse US society. By the year 2050, just over 50% of the US population will be Caucasian, compared with over 70% today. A similar pattern can be expected in the government workforce. Leadership of a diverse society and workforce requires a perspective and a set of skills too many leaders lack today. Managing diversity is not just a nice thing to do; it is a business necessity. While the US Government has been conducting training for leaders for some time in this area, the focus has been on affirmative action, equal employment opportunity, and valuing others. These are important, but they are not enough. We must help our government's leaders create institutions, including systems, processes, and policies which support the development and contributions of all members of the workforce and society. Within the OEMD we are building both stand-alone training programmes on managing diversity and integrating diversity skills into the core programmes that we offer.

## Building international skills

Managing diversity is important internationally as well. A recent survey of OEMD programme participants revealed that 28% supervise or manage foreign nationals working abroad and another 28% offer or market programmes and services to other countries. Forty-nine per cent travel outside the US for business purposes while 47% work with representatives of other countries. Another 47% study and act on issues with international implications. As we develop governmental leaders to manage diversity within our society and workplaces, we must also develop them to succeed internationally. The OEMD already has a global perspectives theme to its curriculum; but the numbers uncovered by our survey have and are increasing dramatically. Subsequently, we must strengthen our executives' knowledge of international affairs and their capability for cross-cultural effectiveness. And, we must expand our international customer base by accepting and exchanging international participants in our programmes. We need to grow our global perspectives theme and become knowledge leaders on international activity for our public service leaders.

OEMD currently has working relationships with Northern Ireland, Bahrain, and Australia, and their government executives have been frequent participants in our LDS programme. We need to pursue additional participation from other parts of the world such as Latin America, Africa, Eastern Europe, Russia and China. We believe our programmes can be useful to their government executives, and we know their executives bring a great deal to our own nation's leaders. We are seeking funding to offer more scholarships for participants to jump-start such arrangements, and we are enhancing our global perspectives theme with new courses and workshops on global trends, negotiations, collaboration, peace-keeping, and international leadership.

53

### Competencies for the 21st century

OPM is also working hard to anticipate the specific nature of work skills and competencies needed for leaders in the 21st century. We are collaborating with our Chief Information Officers Council, the Chief Financial Officers Council, the Acquisition Community, and others to help them redefine the competencies needed for their professions to remain effective and current in this fast-paced global economy. We are also helping them to identify innovative ways of obtaining these new skills. These same reviews are necessary to ensure that our ECQs remain as up-to-date as possible so that our executives can appropriately lead these highly skilled workers.

### Learning technology

In January 1999, President Clinton issued an Executive Order on using technology to improve training opportunities for federal government employees. Spurred by the belief that most federal employees will need specialised training to handle the challenges of the next decade, a technology taskforce has been formed to identify issues and evaluate possible options that will provide better and more accessible learning opportunities to every federal employee through the effective use of technology. OPM has been leading the taskforce in this effort and it has provided us with the opportunity to get agencies to focus more on training in their strategic plans. Another indicator of the importance accorded learning technology was the introduction of HR 4232 in the 2nd Session of the 106th Congress, April 2000: this legislation would provide for the establishment of a programme under which the government would furnish a home computer and Internet access to each of its employees, at no cost to the employee, and able to be used for other purposes.

The acceleration of the use of learning technologies enables agencies more readily to train their geographically dispersed workforces and provide real time-skills development and knowledge enhancement to meet this rapid pace of change and prevent skill obsolescence. It will enable agencies to deliver sophisticated, technologically advanced learning to IT professionals and other technical specialists who must keep pace with the constantly changing, highly complex requirements of their occupations. The taskforce is considering such options as establishing a training technology steering committee and a training technology resource centre which will provide information and promote learning technology.

The issue for OEMD is how to maintain the quality of its programming – so much of which is dependent on building relationships and networks among executives – and still use technology to provide greater access and timely learning. Research has shown that learning technology is not appropriate for all forms and types of learning. Yet, increasing demands on executives' time and the

54

need for greater access to technology places tremendous pressures on training groups to find alternative means for delivering effective development programmes.

### Training and development flexibilities

OPM is continually striving to identify new flexibilities for training and development. It has recently developed legislation to permit agencies to pay the cost of academic degrees when such training is provided by an accredited school and meets an identified agency need. Currently, agencies can pay for degree training related to shortage category positions only. An additional legislative proposal would allow agencies to pay the cost of employees' licenses, certificates and other professional credentials. Both proposals would give agencies additional flexibility to help address recruitment or retention problems and provide necessary training for improving the talents and skills of their employees. However, often these types of options are under-utilised. In particular, for a number of years agencies have had the authority to establish tuition assistance and reimbursement programmes. These are programmes that pay some or all of the costs of college courses. They provide federal employees with opportunities to round out their academic backgrounds and broaden their technical or professional knowledge. Yet, many agencies have failed to fully exploit these opportunities with their leaders and employees.

A recent executive order will allow agencies to use these existing flexibilities in a creative and exciting way. It allows for options and recommendations for establishing an individual training account for each federal worker to use for training relevant to his or her federal employment, using existing resources. Options include giving employees money and time for learning. OPM is piloting this concept with a number of agencies and organisations, including the Retirement and Insurance Service, which provides an account of dollars and time for each employee to allow access to mentors and other forms of self-development. More pilots need to be conducted and results shared with all agencies in order to take full advantage of the flexibilities available to all federal employees.

### 6. Conclusion

OPM leadership and management development programmes and initiatives are designed to support the firm belief that our federal government's most valuable asset is the talented and diverse men and women who work every day to make a difference in the lives of the American people they serve. To this end, OPM has established the OERM and the OEMD to identify, select and develop government leaders whose commitment to public policy and administration transcends their commitment to a specific agency mission or an individual profession. Our executives are being provided with a clear understanding of the competencies required to be successful public service leaders. They also have development programmes, opportunities, and flexibilities to help them maintain continuously a "corporate" view of government with values grounded in the fundamental ideals of our Constitution. These values embrace the dynamics of American democracy and an approach to governance that provides an ongoing vehicle for change within the federal government to meet the challenges of today's world economy and global marketplace.

# Chapter 4

# Staff Development and Training for Leadership in the German Federal Administration*

## 1. Introduction

### The importance of leadership training

The efficient, citizen-oriented and "activating" state has become the vision for the modernisation of the public sector in Germany. The instruments are modern staff development, the use of business methods, and a comprehensive review of tasks. The leading staff in the federal administration have to own and promote all measures that contribute to the goal attainment; they have to act as change agents. In particular, personalities are needed in upper level management who think beyond organisational borders and responsibilities and who use the lessons learned as guidelines for their own general administration activity and policy advice. This means that the central tasks of the modernisation of the state include:

- to support the development of specific leadership qualities of top managers through appropriate measures;
- to prepare future managers for their tasks in a systematic way.

### Selection and promotion of future leaders within the framework of staff development

In Germany, there is no formal procedure to select a pool of future leaders at an early stage like the fast stream in the United Kingdom. Rather, the selection of future managers takes place within the general process of staff development. Thus, it may extend over several years of the career development of future managers. This has advantages and disadvantages:

- Advantage: The selection process is not limited to the early stages of the career process, also "late starters" have the chance for advancement.

---

\* This paper was prepared and presented to the OECD HRM meeting in July 2000 by Dr. Joachim Vollmuth, Head of Division, EU and International Affairs of the Public Service, Federal Ministry of the Interior.

57

- Disadvantage: Specific supportive programmes cannot be provided for the future leading staff in an early stage of their career to the same extent.

Taking into account this starting point, the paper will continue to give an overview on the goals and instruments of general staff development.

## 2. Framework and instruments of staff development

At the federal level, many ministries and agencies have developed concepts and guidelines for staff development. In the following sections, the basic features will be described briefly.

### Objectives and legal framework of staff development

Staff development aims at the systematic and targeted improvement of the knowledge and competencies of employees by considering their professional needs. Staff development should enable each employee to fulfil the tasks of a concrete job as well as planned future uses as best as possible. Therefore, the present professional skills and capabilities, as well as opportunities for personal development have to be considered.

Staff development takes place within a predefined legal framework of the public service. Legal provisions governing civil service careers contain an important and comprehensive set of regulations defining conditions to enter the public service, the career categories, conditions for the promotion to a higher category, etc. The booklet "The Public Service in Germany" published by the Federal Ministry of the Interior gives information on the basic issues.

### Instruments of staff development

#### Systematic introduction and induction of new staff

The relevance of a systematic introduction and induction of new staff is widely underestimated. This is an important leadership task of direct superiors. The new colleagues also have to accept part of the responsibility because of the frequency, duration and intensity of contacts. A "tutor" chosen from among the division staff supports the superior in the introduction and induction. In order to avoid undesirable frictions the predecessors are involved as well.

The newcomers to the civil service have to take part in an obligatory training programme, which is organised by the federal government departments in co-operation with the Federal Academy for Public Administration. The Academy was founded in 1968 as the central training institution for the higher civil service of the Federation. The programme lasts a total of six weeks and is split over the civil servant's first three years in the federal administration. It includes the following phases:

- sector- or agency-specific introductions, seminars "tasks and functioning of federal ministries or agencies" (orientation phase);

- teaching programmes "basic knowledge and framework of general administrative activity", economics, public law, budget management (inter-disciplinary co-operation);

- seminars "training and team work", "leadership and co-operation" (promotion of key qualifications).

### Staff development planning

Staff development planning is a core task of the personnel administration. The purpose is to analyse the staff situation in every department or agency and the consequences for staff development every year and to consult with the staff representatives. The objective is a demand-driven career planning of employees.

An important goal is to promote generalists. As ministries have complex tasks and often new programmes employees are needed who are highly qualified and, at the same time, variable and flexible. Thus, a narrow specialisation is suitable only for employees with jobs with clearly delimited special functions. Otherwise, civil servants will normally be expected to accept and to give up current tasks and to learn new skills and techniques. This includes working abroad, for example, in an international organisation. This readiness to change is not only expected from younger but also from colleagues at a later stage in their career.

In order to promote the leadership qualities of future managers of the public service the newcomers to the first category are in general employed on the level of public agencies. Here they have the opportunity to get practical leadership and management experience at an early stage of their career.

### Personnel dialogue

In order to improve co-operative leadership and staff development special interviews are held by superiors with the staff members at least once a year. They are used to make a diagnosis of the performance of the staff member as well as of the prospects of development and promotion. Qualification, service-related behaviour and performance are discussed and measured with regard to agreed goals. The objective is to show how to maintain and improve levels of performance. The professional goals, wishes and plans of staff, as well as development opportunities, are an important part of the interview.

59

*Training*

Training is a central element of staff development. The goal is to improve the effectiveness of the work and to qualify for "higher posts", in particular leadership positions. As mentioned before, the Federal Academy for Public Administration is in charge of preparing and implementing such programmes. Its training programmes include a broad range of professional and task-specific seminars and courses, developed and adapted in consultation with the departments and agencies every year.

The programme design at the Federal Academy is increasingly determined by the objective to increase the level of competencies of participants to a measurable extent. This means that the development programmes must not be a variety of single programmes but they rather have to be integrated into a systematic qualification programme. The goal is to get a series of programmes that build upon each other like building blocks.

Also, the contents and methods have to be in line with needs profiles which have to be defined by the demand side (ministries and agencies) and which have to take into account specific functions (*e.g.* head of section) and sectors (organisation, law making, etc.). Then the key qualifications have to be deduced from the definition of knowledge and competencies, which are necessary for the optimal management of the respective tasks and responsibilities. The training measures have to be designed with regard to the typical gap between the core competencies and the present skills and qualifications.

A further consequence is that the participation at specific training programmes within certain periods is obligatory and linked to personnel decisions (job rotation, promotion, etc.).

In response to present needs the programme of the Federal Academy focuses on the following tasks and responsibilities:

- leadership training and training of future managers;
- important cross-cutting functions: personnel, organisation, budget, IT, reporting;
- law making;
- international activities, foreign languages; and
- competency in European matters.

*Evaluation procedures for personnel decisions*

The goals of staff development imply that the civil servants, their superiors and the HRM department have as much information as possible about the capacity, capability and performance of each staff member. In this regard, the evaluation system is of crucial relevance. In addition to this, differentiated and reliable personnel evaluations make personnel decisions transparent and acceptable for everybody.

Personnel evaluation must fulfil different functions: it provides a tool for career planning as well as information to get an estimate of the development potential for future uses. Therefore, it includes two dimensions:

- past performance; and
- evaluation of future competencies and suitable uses.

Evaluation in these areas is based on different evaluation criteria:

- performance evaluation:
  - work results: quality and usability, quantity of work and meeting deadlines, ratio of "inputs" with regard to output;
  - professional knowledge: up-to-date and soundness;
  - working method: initiative, representation of working area, service-orientation;
  - social competence: willingness to accept responsibility, reliability, behaviour in conflict situations;
  - leadership: organisation, delegation, motivation, support of staff, etc.
- evaluation of competence and future uses:
  - capability to comprehend;
  - capability to make sound judgements and to think;
  - decision-making capability and capability to assert oneself;
  - conceptual work;
  - ability to put up with stress;
  - ability to express orally and in writing;
  - organisational skills, etc.

*Transparent selection decisions through advertising posts for promotion*

In order to guarantee equal opportunity and transparency ex-post control of personnel related decisions all posts are advertised in general. It is possible to deviate from this practice only in special cases according to predefined criteria and with the agreement of staff representatives. In the case of external recruitment for available posts and in particular for the promotion in higher ranks, there are special procedural requirements. In general, an assessment procedure is obligatory. This is supposed to check the professional and personal qualification of a candidate, including his social competence in a kind of assessment centre.

61

### Further work on staff development methods

This was a brief description of existing concepts of staff development. The activities related to the modernisation of the state in Germany focus on the further development of the concepts as well as on implementation measures, both at the federal level and the level of the *Bundesländer*. The federal government has established a cross departmental working group for this work. In its report of I November this group provides a new instrument of capacity development. The evaluation of the superior's performance done by their staff. The constructive criticism of staff members shall stimulate the superiors to reflect their leadership methods and to initiate improvements.

## 3.    Examples of leadership training

### Leadership training at the federal level

The necessity for a systematic leadership training was a major reason for the foundation of the Federal Academy of Public Administration. It has been in existence for more than 30 years, and has continuously developed this central pillar and elaborated a four-phase system of leadership development.

Today's programmes are based on the recognition that the specific challenges to the managers make it necessary for them to acquire new key competencies in order to fulfil their functions as change agents in the framework of modernisation and reform of government and public administration. The so-called "soft skills" (social, strategic and change management competencies) should enable managers to think in terms of strategic and network structures and to guide and motivate their staff towards results-oriented work through a co-operative leadership style and appropriate instruments (*e.g.*, team work, personnel dialogue, delegation).

The four-phase system of leadership training of the Federal Academy works as follows:

- Phase 1: **Competency training for future managers**
  - leadership and communication competencies for future managers (negotiations, rhetoric, personality profile), intensive training in communication, co-operation, teamwork.
- Phase 2: **Qualification for leadership tasks** – four-week courses to train leaders with the following objectives:
  - knowledge and capabilities for the management and direction of autonomous organisation units;
  - leadership drawing on psychology, organisational theory and social sciences;

– analysis of own work and leadership behaviour;

– simulation programmes: computer based simulation of administrative decisions;

– follow-up seminars:

  • work organisation and stress situations;

  • time management;

  • media training for television and radio;

  • knowledge management;

  • change management within administrative modernisation;

  • personnel development in private enterprises.

• Phase 3: **Development of advanced leadership skills** (experienced managers):

  – three week internship in the private sector;

  – training to enhance European competence and international co-operation;

  – follow-up seminar, *e.g.*:

    • personality and success in leadership;

    • managing work groups, teams and project teams;

    • managing dialogue and negotiations.

• Phase 4: **Special knowledge and exchange of experience** (top management):

  – forum of directors/presidents;

  – media training for television and radio;

  – individual coaching for top and senior positions;

  – leadership for leaders.

In the context of the modernisation of the state an interesting development can be observed. There is an increasing demand for training and consultancy which is to be integrated into comprehensive in-house projects of ministries or agencies concerning staff development or organisational restructuring. The services of the Federal Academy include:

  • the definition of goals;

  • the quantitative and qualitative analysis of training needs;

  • methodological recommendations;

  • individual contract and financial management with specific consultants, including advising contractors during the implementation process (*e.g.* introduction of a new personnel evaluation system in a ministry, including consulting on new performance agreements, the design of evaluation sheets and explanations).

63

Another trend is the arrangement of subject-specific workshops for practitioners working on similar reform projects. What practitioners ask for is a focused, professionally directed forum for the exchange of experiences based on "learning from best practice" and "benchmarking" methods.

### Leadership training on the level of the Bundesländer

The Bundesländer have developed different concepts for their leadership training. The models for a long-term training of future leading staff are of particular interest. This paper describes very briefly the following models:

- the Leadership Academy in Baden-Württemberg;
- the Civil Service Leadership College Speyer.

It has to be added that concepts of long-term leadership training have also been developed and implemented by other Bundesländer, e.g. Bavaria.

#### The Leadership Academy Baden-Württemberg

Admission and course:

- Fifteen-month course for up to 20 participants from government and up to 10 external participants; organisation: three months basic course work/three months internship in a private enterprise/four months intensive studies/three months internship in a foreign administration/one month final conclusion.
- Participants are granted special leave and are seconded to the Leadership Academy.
- Conditions to enter: evaluations above-average, time spent in public service: three to five years on two posts.
- Participants are deemed to be future managers, the average age being 36 years.
- Selection of participants: proposals by superiors or personal application.
- Selection through assessment centres, evaluation by senior civil servants.
- No legal guarantee for promotion after the leadership training.

Thematic design:

- Personality development (competency framework for managers, self assessment, feed back); work in self-driven interdisciplinary teams/projects, conflict management, coaching, supervision.
- Instruments of personnel and organisation development: strategic planing, decision making, methods of leadership, quality management, project management, techniques of presentation and negotiation, personnel dialogue, management by objectives, organisation analysis, value analysis, European competence, international negotiation, intercultural training, IT.

- In compliance with the concept of the government of Baden-Württemberg "Training 2001" participants will be trained in various thematic fields to be supporters for the processes of change in the public administration. They shall promote the transfer of knowledge between public administration, politics, economy and social groups.

Constraints for reaching the goals:

- The fact that future managers are free from the service on the one hand allows them to concentrate on the training. On the other side disadvantages can derive from the fact that the training programme up to now is not a part of a consequent system of career planning, which builds on successful participation in the training and opens up clear career perspectives for participants. Participants are not assured of later promotion. If there are no promising career offers afterwards this naturally can lead to frustration.

## The Civil Service Leadership College Speyer

Admission and course:

- Sixteen course weeks in 2.5 years, followed by an internship. Organisation: basic course work and project-related courses, practical exercises and "fireplace talks" under the direction of scientific staff of the German Post-Graduate School of Administrative Sciences Speyer.

- The participants remain active civil servants in their posts and continue to fulfil their duties, but their superiors must agree to their participation in six weeks of courses per year.

- Conditions to enter: above-average evaluations; time spent in civil service: seven years; required rank: A15 or A16.

- Participants currently in leadership positions or will shortly obtain leadership functions; the average age is 40 years.

- Selection of participants: proposals by superiors or personal application.

- Selection through the Conference of the Secretaries of State of the participating states.

- No legal guarantee for promotion after the end of the leadership programme.

Thematic design:

- The main thematic fields of leadership training of the Civil Service Leadership College Speyer are similar to those of the Leadership Academy Baden-Württemberg, *e.g.* instruments of personnel and organisation development/planing and decision-making/budgeting and controlling/ politics and public administration/EU-competence. The programme in

65

detail is related to the working field of the participants in many regards and opens up a lot of new perspectives. Comparative analysis of other administrative systems, particularly in foreign countries, shall enable the participants to reflect critically on the traditional structures of their own administrative work.

Constraints for reaching the goals:

• The leadership training of the Civil Service Leadership College Speyer is characterised by a permanent change of seminar weeks and ongoing service duties for the participants. On the one hand, this brings about a lot of additional stress for the participants. On the other side the practical relevance of the training is more evident.

• The training is targeted to enable the participants to take over leading positions in the public administration. Its aim at human resources development, however, would require a clear linkage to a consequent system of career planning which opens up clear career perspectives for the participants. The Civil Service Leadership College Speyer clearly points out that in this respect a lot has still to be done. It will be of crucial relevance whether the activities to develop the concepts and promote their implementation mentioned above achieve progress in this respect.

## 4. Conclusion

In summary, it can be said that both leadership programmes have made great efforts to develop an effective training programme for future leading staff in the public service. The ambitious approach necessarily causes questions and problems for the practical implementation, particularly with regard to staff development and career planing in the ministries and administrative bodies. These issues still have to be dealt with in future development work.

As mentioned above, the establishment of the cross-departmental working group on staff development concepts and implementation at the federal level as well as the *Bundesländer* level will be an important tool in shaping this future development.

Chapter 5

# Leadership Development Strategy in Sweden*

## 1. Introduction

All work in Swedish public administration[1] must stem from three fundamental principles: democracy, the rule of law and efficiency. Democracy requires public administration to perform its tasks in accordance with the decisions taken by Parliament and the government. The rule of law means that public administration must make correct decisions on the basis of current laws and other statutory regulations, and individuals must also have a chance of getting their cases heard in court. Efficiency demands that public administration bring about the intended results and attain the objectives laid down by the government, and do so cost-effectively.

In Sweden, development and revisions are underway in public administration to ensure that its functions are performed at a sophisticated level of service, with transparency and public access to information, competent managers and a greater capacity for change. This paper describes the Swedish Government's view of leadership in the state and its strategies for obtaining effective leadership.

### Delegation of responsibility

Since the mid-1980s, the Swedish state has been highly decentralised. The state, *i.e.* the central government administration, comprises the government and Government Offices, the judiciary and the central agencies. The latter are accountable to the government as a whole, but each is subordinate to a ministry. Responsibility has been delegated and deregulated, to enhance both internal and external efficiency. The trend has been for the state to move from regulatory governance and control towards the formulation of objectives for activities and monitoring of performance.

The government has delegated much of its employer policy to the agencies. Agency heads are thus responsible for their respective agencies' employer policy,

---

* This paper was prepared by Dr. Monica Wåglund, Director of Development, National Council for Quality and Development.

*i.e.* matters relating to staff and managerial recruitment, skills development and mobility, and conditions of pay and employment. The central government employer policy is aimed at generating forms of organisation, control and management that are conducive to the three fundamental values of democracy, the rule of law and efficiency permeating the whole of public administration.

The reason why the agencies themselves are responsible for employer policy is that the agencies are supposed to use employer policy as a means of attaining the aims of their activities, in a highly efficient manner that inspires citizens' confidence. The government's task is to impose relevant requirements, and to follow up the agencies' employer policy.

For employer policy to be effective, it needs to be adapted to the requirements of the activities concerned. This includes familiarising employees with the objectives of their activities and ensuring that they enjoy good working conditions, and that their skills are developed and their experience utilised.

### Control

Parliament and the government have three important instruments for controlling public administration:

- the power of legislation;
- the power of the purse;
- the power of appointment.

Exercising the power of the purse stems from the agencies' budget documentation. This is examined in detail by the ministries concerned and the Ministry of Finance. The outcome is the Government's Budget and Finance Bill each spring, proposing various spending limits for policy areas, and the subsequent autumn Budget and Finance Bill, on which Parliament must decide. The more detailed resolutions concerning the objectives of activities and instructions to the agencies pursuant to the government budget decided upon are contained in the government's official documents placing appropriations at the disposal of the agencies concerned. The agencies' annual reports to the respective ministries are important instruments in the government's follow-up work. The government also controls activities through its choice of chairman and members of the agencies' boards.

Since the government's power of appointment is a key instrument for controlling public administration, it appoints agency heads. However, one precondition for workable government control is the existence of a carefully considered and implemented policy on managerial recruitment. The skills and leadership of managers largely determine the government's success in implementing its policy.

The government's performance management of the agencies has entailed fewer rules prescribing *how* activities are to be conducted. By the same token, it has imposed greater demands on the agencies, through their accountable freedom to choose their methods of attaining objectives. The government's premise is that the person an agency has appointed to direct an activity should also have the authority to head the choice of instruments and means of attaining its targets.

## 2. Importance of leadership

In its manager policy, the government formulates its view of the agency head's role as follows:

*An agency head must have ample knowledge of the specialist area of the agency concerned, with an overall grasp of its work. Heading a central-government agency also presupposes numerous other important qualities. The head must be skilled in co-operating with his principal, in the form of the Government and respective ministry. Being able to analyse, take decisions and assume responsibility for decisions is also required. In addition, the head must be capable of communicating with other stakeholders, including – not least – the public and the mass media. Linguistic skills and general competence for international work are becoming ever more important, especially in view of Sweden's EU membership.*

*Fundamentally, what the role requires is leadership skill – the ability to put across the objectives adopted for activities, to delegate, and to inspire subordinates' commitment to and enthusiasm for the work in attaining the objectives. What makes a manager a true leader is this very ability to mobilise other people's efforts and lay the foundations of their high motivation and enjoyment of the work.*

Agency heads are required to direct activities in accordance with the government's intentions, and these include vigorous regeneration efforts. The heads are also intended to re-examine and assign new priorities for activities, and to find opportunities through measures to enhance efficiency, achieve rationalisation, and boost productivity. The agencies' great freedom to choose their own forms of work thus imposes particular demands on their heads.

Most important of all are:

- skilled leadership;
- the ability to present and obtain a hearing for the agency's aims;
- delegation of responsibility;
- the capacity to command enthusiasm and inspire employees to make a concerted effort to attain objectives.

The characteristic of a true leader is, according to the government's policy, the ability to induce people to feel highly motivated for and committed to their work.

The regeneration and development work under way in Swedish public administration depends on good leadership and creative employees alike. For this reason, it is important to cultivate and help to promote the kinds of working conditions in the agencies that enable creativity to develop. By this means, public administration characterised by the fundamental values of democracy, the rule of law and efficiency can be achieved.

Getting hold of the right person for the job as agency head is a key task. The Government Offices seek candidates both inside and outside the agency sphere. Since major change is taking place in the wider society, public administration also requires managers with experience of business and other sectors. These managers must have a chance to devote themselves to the particular requirements that govern the work of public administration.

A survey carried out several years ago shows that the average Swedish director-general is in most cases a man aged about 55, with a university degree in law, economics or the social sciences and has spent virtually all his working life in central government. The government is making a particular effort to increase the numbers of female agency heads, people with experience of other sectors of society and employees with a non-Swedish background. The proportion of female agency heads has risen over the past few years. Mobility among agency heads has been considerably enhanced over the past decade, and the government will continue henceforth to work for natural mobility among agency heads.

## 3. Strategies for leadership development

The government regards managerial recruitment as vitally important to public administration, and considers that it should receive more attention at all administrative levels. The recruitment of agency heads is subject to the government's overall recruitment policy adopted in the mid-1990s. This policy identifies the following key aspects:

- professional recruitment;
- more women in managerial positions;
- good induction programmes;
- continuous development of managers' skills;
- performance dialogues;
- mobility.

### Recruitment

Following consultations with the Cabinet Office and Ministry of Justice, every ministry is responsible for recruiting agency heads in its own sphere. For universities and colleges, recruitment of vice-chancellors and principals takes place according to the proposals put forward by the higher education institution concerned. In these cases, there is thus no special recruitment procedure in the Government Offices.

A written schedule of requirements, based on the agency's current and future activities, must always be drawn up before the quest for candidates begins. Particular emphasis should be laid on leadership qualities and previous managerial experience. A wide-ranging search procedure means that the government seeks candidates from the business sector, municipalities and county councils as well.

### Female candidates

As far as possible, there should always be a female candidate on the shortlist. The aim of recruiting managers who are as highly qualified as possible in public administration should be attained by using the skills possessed by both men and women.

### Induction

Newly appointed managers must be given both individually adapted and general induction.

Great care should be devoted to induction programmes to ensure that they lay the foundations for constructive and smooth co-operation. General induction routines must exist at every ministry, while the individually adapted induction should include, for example, a meeting with the ministry management in the form of an initial performance dialogue.

The Government Offices arrange general, joint induction seminars for newly appointed agency heads. These seminars are aimed at clarifying demands and expectations with respect to the role of head, and at developing the managers' capacity for leadership in public administration.

### Leadership training

Leadership training in various forms must be offered to new and established agency heads alike.

Agency heads who have undergone induction training are offered the opportunity for further leadership training in small groups. The purpose of these is for participants to engage with colleagues in open discussions of current issues relating to the managerial role. Theme seminars on such general issues are arranged where necessary, and are attended also by representatives of the ministries' political management.

Also included in leadership training is the opportunity for individual inputs to hone managers' skills in order for them to develop the specialist expertise that particular agency heads may need.

### Performance dialogues

A regular performance dialogue between the ministry management and agency head is a supplementary control instrument for the government within the framework of the normal budget process.

This dialogue normally comprises two parts. During the first part, the matters dealt with are the objectives of the work, results attained, effects, and costs. In connection with these, the ministry management should clarify and define more precisely the objectives adopted by the government for the agency's work.

The second part of the dialogue takes the form of an individual planning discussion between the agency head and the cabinet minister or state secretary. During this part of the discussion, matters covered include the manager's work situation and needs for development and change.

Regular performance dialogues should normally be held with the agency heads on an annual basis.

### Mobility

Mobility in the managerial post promotes both the agency's efficiency and managers' personal development. Increased mobility also makes changes in and removals from the post less dramatic, and encourages alternations between managerial and other duties to be seen as natural.

Appointments for limited periods should be used as an instrument both to promote mobility between different duties and assignments and to remove agency heads from office where necessary. New appointments for agency heads should be for a six-year period with re-appointments at a maximum of three years.

Unless already included in a performance dialogue, the cabinet minister or state secretary should hold a planning discussion with the agency head not later than six months before the end of the appointment period.

In every ministry, there should be smoothly functioning routines for monitoring and planning both short- and long-term appointments of agency heads.

### Managerial recruitment and leadership training below the agency-head level

Mobility among managers below the level of head is low. The work of recruiting new staff at this level is most appropriately a function for the agencies themselves to perform, given their responsibility and powers. Thus, agency heads themselves appoint their own immediate colleagues. However, in certain cases – owing to the scale or particular significance of the activities concerned – the government may choose to appoint a senior director who belongs to the executive committee and is also the director-general's deputy.

The agencies also have scope for developing some form of employer co-operation within the framework of the National Agency for Government Employers, for the purpose of bringing about greater mobility. The essential purpose of increased mobility is to attain the correct balance between continuity and renewal in activities.

Performance dialogues held by the ministry management with their agency heads can provide them with valuable information about qualified managers with good leader qualities within the agency who could be used in some post as agency head, or in some other leading position in public administration.

Agency heads are expected to follow the government's policy for managerial recruitment and leadership training within their agencies, and give due attention to the same key aspects. Thus great care is devoted firstly to the recruitment process. Not infrequently, the agencies draw on external support from professional recruitment consultants, especially in small agencies where this recruitment takes place relatively seldom. In larger agencies, staff may be employed with the specific function of recruiting managers. Agency heads are usually involved themselves in the selection process. The local trade union representatives also often have the opportunity of playing a particular part in the process by meeting potential candidates and carrying out interviews. The agencies are generally aware that managerial recruitment is extremely important to the success of their activities, since it affects so many other people's commitment to, and enjoyment of, their work at the agency.

After an appointment, and especially if the new manager is externally recruited, some form of induction programme is offered. Large agencies may have their own training programmes for new managers, while smaller ones can combine induction of a new manager with the offer to use some external leadership programme that is available on the market.

Agencies' approaches to continuous leadership training vary somewhat. The usual arrangement is for the agency's management to arrange special seminars on matters relating to the role of manager and leader, or on current issues concerning the function of developing activities. External support and assistance are the norm for these seminars. One example of such development inputs may be training to carry out personal developmental interviews with employees. Annual managerial discussions on activity planning and development are another example of such measures.

73

As far as resources permit (and this normally applies only to large and medium-sized agencies) more extensive training programmes are held at more or less regular intervals, with external assistance. These programmes are either devised internally or purchased from consulting firms, with the executive management as the purchaser – in both cases, often with the close involvement of the agency head and management. Management consultants and others with skills in the areas concerned are engaged for the implementation. In large agencies where the managerial group may comprise a total of 50 people or more, advanced training programmes may be ordered from external providers. These may be universities or colleges with special researchers and teachers in the field of, for example, organisational development. The type of large-scale training programme that extends over several months, or up to a year, may be part of a more comprehensive remoulding of activities and may serve as preparation for the managers' leadership tasks.

Management-training inputs are thus delegated to the agency concerned, just like other aspects of responsibility for employer policy. What has previously been lacking are special training programmes that, first, lay emphasis on the particular function of being a manager in public administration and, secondly, provide scope for the exchange of experience between agencies. Moreover, the smaller agencies – and most agencies in public administration are fairly small – have very limited scope for drawing up or ordering advanced training programmes: the resources allocated do not permit them to do so. This deficiency, coupled with the importance attached by the government in its administrative policy to managers in public administration having access to needs-oriented training programmes, was one reason for the formation of the National Council for Quality and Development.

## 4. Leadership training: National Council for Quality and Development

The government set up the Council in 1999 with the function, in the interest of the public, to support and stimulate work on quality development and the supply of skills in central-government administration. It is intended to encourage and facilitate the agencies' work on systematically developing overall quality in their activities. Another aim of the Council is to support central government administration in its efforts to acquire, develop and retain the right skills.

One key task for the Council is to assist in recruiting and training managers in public administration. The Council is currently running various types of management-training programmes, several of which are described here in more detail.

### Strategic management

This programme concerns the task of leadership, future trends and activity development in the dynamic environment in which the central government agencies operate. The training is intended to contribute to personal skills enhancement through analysis of international trends, a comprehensive approach and the ability to adopt a focus and direct changes in complex organisations. The participants are intended to develop a more sound and thoroughly based understanding of:

- the agencies' conditions in the form of political, social and economic factors in the surrounding world;
- the consequences of the internationalisation of the agency world;
- the role and responsibility of public administration within the framework of a democratic system.

The intention is also for participants to develop their skills in:

- assessing the scope for shaping, developing and attaining efficiency in agency activities;
- developing methods of analysing activities;
- identifying opportunities for development;
- initiating and directing developmental work at an overall level.

The programme is designed for managers and senior officials at the level immediately below the agency heads in medium-sized or large agencies. It comprises eight seminars lasting for a total of 24 days, spread over one year.

### Programme for female managers

This programme caters for female managers with their own responsibility for activities and staff. It is intended to help in developing the participants' personal, social, professional and functional skills, thereby boosting their managerial expertise.

Its purposes include the following:

- to encourage more women in managerial positions to apply for the top management posts at central government agencies;
- to thereby increase the representation of women in management;
- to create new interfaces and networks between agencies.

The aim is that, by the time the programme is concluded, at least half the participants will have obtained, or be on the way to obtaining, senior posts.

The programme comprises a total of 25 days and includes five seminar blocks, four separate supervision sessions, individual career consultation and a working trip.

### Mentor programme

This programme caters for relatively recently appointed middle managers.

Managerial development through mentorship is a process in which two people are deliberately brought together to learn from each other in working for an agreed objective. Each manager (adept) is assigned a personal mentor, and the mentor and adept devise a form of co-operation on equal terms.

The programme aims to:

- promote the participants' personal and professional development in their managerial roles;

- enable each participant to obtain support from, and compare notes with, a person qualified to serve as a sounding board;

- develop new networks;

- generate opportunities for mutual learning.

The programme runs for just over a year, comprising seven whole-day and two half-day courses. It starts with a half-day induction for adepts and mentors in which they are presented to the other participants, review their own expectations, and gain a clear understanding of the roles of adept and mentor, and of how the programme is designed to work. The purpose of this occasion is to give all the participants a chance to become acquainted, and also to describe mentorship as a method and the ways in which one can work to attain the expected results.

During the ensuing year, adept and mentors meet in a way they decide for themselves and, in addition, on certain prescribed training days. Officially, the programme ends with several whole-day courses at the end of the year.

There has proved to be great interest among older and more experienced managers in serving as mentors for their younger colleagues.

Besides the above-mentioned programmes, Sweden will join in providing participants for a couple of joint European programmes.

## Note

1. The term "public administration" is used throughout to refer to central-government administration, and excludes administration at municipal level.

Chapter 6

# Manager and Management Development in Norway*

## 1. Introduction

In 1992, the former Ministry of Government Administration, in co-operation with the Directorate of Public Management, prepared a strategy for public administration development for the period 1993-1995. The principal point of departure was the Report to the Storting No. 35 (1991-1992) "The Central Government's Administration and Personnel Policies". The Ministry of Labour and Government Administration decided to continue this strategy work for the period 1998-2002.

The Directorate of Public Management holds the main central government responsibility for various manager development measures and for assistance in connection with management development in government agencies.

The strategy for development of managers and management presented here was prepared on the basis of recommendations made by personnel managers. A fundamental assumption has been that competence-building for managers and other employees is an important component of the further development of an efficient, user-friendly, quality-conscious and well-organised public administration. Emphasis has been placed on the management's responsibility for carrying out development work of this kind.

The elected political leadership (in the ministries) and the various executive managers in government agencies have different tasks. This paper does not deal with development measures for political leadership and government roles, but concerns only the executive management roles. It is addressed to managers with line responsibility in both ministries and external agencies. That is to say, top managers, front-line managers, and middle managers, of whom there are currently 10 000 in Norway. Overall, it is intended to provide help and support for managers, personnel department staff and other key persons involved in leadership development at both central and local levels in Norwegian administration.

---

* This paper was prepared by Finn Melbø and Turid Semb. Mr Melbø is the Deputy Director General of the Ministry of Labour and Government Administration. Mr. Semb is an adviser in the Ministry.

A distinction is made in this paper between manager development, which relates to the knowledge and skills of individual managers in exercising the role of manager, and management development, which concerns the systems for management and control of agencies. Strengthening of management is viewed as essential to the development of the individual manager and *vice versa* .

## 2.  Importance of leadership

### *Manager and management development: goals and requirements*

In the Civil Service, managers are responsible for the employment of their staff and the implementation of development measures. Members of the public demand availability and quality, and are not preoccupied with the issue of which agency provides the service they are interested in. It is therefore important to encourage staff to take an integrated, holistic approach to public administration and to involve them in user-orientation and readjustment work.

The challenges facing Civil Service managers today far exceed those of the traditional senior civil servant with clear statutory responsibility and a clearly defined job description. A major factor of management responsibility is the continuous development taking place in one's own sector. Many agencies are currently facing major readjustment challenges.

### *Management development and manager development*

The terms "management training" and "manager development" are often used as if they were synonymous. In this document management training is subordinate to manager development. Training is only one of a number of measures adopted for development purposes. Management development means a systematic development of the management function in the individual agency and of the systems that provide support for managers, such as financial management, personnel and payroll, information, and environment, health and safety. Managers here are involved in direct and binding interaction with each other with an emphasis on developing teamwork and co-operation across the boundaries of agencies and organisational units within an agency. This particularly requires knowledge of, and insight into, Civil Service instructions and frameworks.

Management development must be based on the concrete demands and challenges faced by an agency. In readjustment work, management development and organisational development are particularly closely connected.

**Manager development** concerns managers as individuals, and is aimed at providing managers with:

- knowledge – full understanding of managerial roles and tasks;
- skills in practical management;

- attitudes that stimulate the resources of staff and colleagues and continually improve the handling of new challenges;
- self-knowledge and self-development – insight into one's own personality and manner, forces that influence one's behaviour, and ways of making improvements;
- social insight concerning staff and colleagues and the ability to use two-way communication skills in exercising leadership ("social intelligence").

In all of these areas, it is important that managers are capable of and predisposed to making improvements and changes.

Manager development measures must be planned in relation to the manager's personal and professional qualifications for the job situation concerned, and in relation to the stage that the manager has reached in his or her career. A managerial role is itself an opportunity for continuous learning. Few other roles provide the same potential for stretching one's capacity to absorb new knowledge and try out skills. However, there is nothing automatic about the acquisition of management skills. Learning can partly be supported by measures in connection with day-to-day work. Examples of this are team-building, feedback systems, peer guidance, mentoring arrangements and courses related to concrete needs. Most of these involve systematic external training.

### Goals of management and manager development

The Report to the Storting No. 35 (1991-1992) established management policy as an important development area. The purpose of management policy in the Civil Service is to promote accountability at all levels and help create an adaptable and user-oriented administration. Management policy is to be realised through measures that encourage:

- development of control systems and management function;
- use of personnel policy instruments for managers.

Management development must be associated with performance requirements and attention to management functions in individual agencies. Concrete goals and methods must be devised locally in the agencies themselves. Systematic development measures should help to strengthen management functions in government agencies to enable the individual agencies to fulfil the requirements regarding:

- goal and performance orientation;
- adaptability;
- stimulation of learning processes;
- orientation towards effective interaction between levels and between sectors.

79

Management development measures must help to safeguard the public sector's platform of values with a particular emphasis on equal treatment, security under the law and predictability, and contribute to a strengthening of transparency in the administration.

Manager development in the Civil Service should largely involve helping managers to define their managerial roles, to make conscious choices when involved in role conflicts or confusion of roles and to strengthen their capacity to exercise leadership. The goal of manager development must be defined in relation to concrete challenges faced by the individual agency and its managers and to the type of development need experienced by the managers.

The Report to the Storting No. 35 (1991-1992) lists a number of principles for persons holding managerial responsibility. Managers have responsibility for:

- meeting existing targets that are of benefit to users and complying with political and executive decisions;
- playing a part in improvement, renewal and readjustment with a view to achieving long-term goals for the administration;
- developing the independence, competence and sense of responsibility of the staff;
- representing the employer and exercising good personnel management;
- safeguarding gender equality considerations;
- developing themselves as leaders.

Manager development measures are intended to help Civil Service managers to meet the overall demands made of them while stimulating them to fulfil their managerial roles as well as possible.

In new phases and situations, needs arise which make the task of strengthening one's own competence a continual challenge and process. That "a person who feels himself a finished manager will soon be finished as a manager" is not just a byword. In relation to the needs of both the individual and the organisation, it is desirable to think of careers in terms of a broader context than the choice between a managerial and a professional career. Provisions should be made for greater flexibility in relation to individual careers both by allowing managers to work in different types of managerial posts during the course of their careers and by allowing them to choose alternatives to managerial work at natural stages during their careers.

### Challenges facing today's leader

Managers of government agencies are required to keep informed about development characteristics in the surrounding community and to detect early signals that may have significance for the agency of which they are in charge. Managers are also expected to be abreast of developments in other sectors than their own so as to sustain a comprehensive view and foster co-ordination.

Development characteristics with particular significance for development of management are:

- Readjustments and major organisational changes: A number of agencies are undergoing changes in their form of association with the state and in their internal structures as well as changes in diversity and complexity. A rapid pace of change must be expected in society in general and in the administration in particular.

- IT developments: New technical solutions increase the pace of change and enable the administration to improve internal functions and the service provided to users and society as a whole. An IT strategy for the government administration will attempt to exploit synergy gains and provide a more unified interface with users.

- Competence-building as a priority area, both of the focus on continuing education and training and of learning through day-to-day work in the agencies. The changes in age distribution in government agencies will result in a need to give priority to training and competence-building for all age groups, not least for older employees.

- Changing labour market. Increasing competition for highly qualified labour at all levels will increase the challenges involved in recruiting staff to government agencies.

- Increased media focus, not least in the public sector.

- Increased internationalisation requires managers both to keep track of developments abroad and to be more closely involved in co-ordinated international action.

- Ethical issues for the administration are being focused on both nationally and internationally.

### The ideal manager

A somewhat demanding portrait of the ideal Civil Service manager can be suggested. Ideally, we need managers who:

- take the lead in showing vision and optimism and who stimulate productivity at all levels;

- take the initiative in making necessary changes and are able both to prepare sound strategies for change and to implement them;

81

- are bridge-builders, who contribute in constructive ways to handling conflicts, creating networks and co-ordinating and helping to solve problems across organisational boundaries;

- are capable of steering, of setting standards, and of assessing, following up and taking responsibility for the results;

- are competent advisers, whose work is both process-oriented and result-oriented;

- inspire and generate energy in those working under them;

- facilitate growth and development for both themselves and their staff;

- foster a sound working environment and adopt a personnel policy that is perceived as fair and where needs for competence-building and readjustment are provided for;

- use information technology as an instrument for both long-term planning and readjustment. The IT competence of the management is important for the effective utilisation of new technology for ordinary operations, for internal and external co-operation, for making readjustments and for achieving synergy;

- are capable of using teamwork to strengthen and supplement the competence of individual members of staff and of promoting development across the boundaries of organisational units, sectors and agencies;

- are able to handle the media.

Few people would be capable of fulfilling all of these requirements, which may, however, be regarded as constituting an ideal to strive after. The challenge is not reduced by the growing variety of participants and agencies, the increasing attention of the media, the tighter control of the public sector and the frequent focus on policy issues in daily work. Demands regarding interpersonal, emotional skills are also increasing.

## 3.   Strategies for leadership development

### Values and main focus for development

In the value platform of the government sector importance is attached to equal treatment, security under the law and predictability. During a period marked by change, the requirements regarding transparency in the administration face many challenges. The purpose of the following points is to draw attention to some of the factors that must be taken into account in planning and implementing measures for managers. The government must give priority to:

- A user-oriented and quality-conscious administration that makes continual efforts to pay attention to the assessments and needs of users. The recipients of services supply valuable information for internal development work in the form of service declarations, constructive feedback and dialogues.
- An administration that views transparency and access to information as intrinsic values. In a democracy, transparency is a precondition for participation and involvement.
- Performance-oriented management must coexist with insight into how results are achieved. Results include services and products, social consequences and user-satisfaction. An important precondition for this is active participation by the staff.
- Communication and interaction between different public bodies, and between different levels of the administration.
- Consideration of, and attitudes towards, dilemmas of Civil Service ethics, which are faced particularly by managers. Communicating openly about ethical dilemmas is an important stage in dealing with them.
- A clearer, more responsible employer role, which applies to the following factors, among others:
  - Competence-building and learning in the organisation. This applies to all phases of life from responsibility for recruiting to senior policy measures that contribute to competence-building throughout a manager's career. Requirements regarding competence-building and lifelong learning must be fulfilled by means of organisational arrangements that promote experiential learning and through participation in courses.
  - Competence to utilise pay and personnel policy instruments and agreements.
  - Promoting and utilising the various personnel resources by means of both recruiting and development measures. During the plan period there must be a determined focus on recruitment of women to senior management posts in the government sector.
  - Handling of an increasing diversity and greater heterogeneity both in the agencies and in society at large. Major factors are ethnic background, composition of sex roles, knowledge and experience.
  - Professional follow-up of and dialogue with staff. The increase in staff competence implies that a co-operative approach to development must be adopted. There must be a strengthening of the independence and sense of responsibility of individual staff members coupled with an open and receptive dialogue with users.

81

- The information function and the need for clarity in the role of manager.

- Work on readjustment. The rapid pace of change requires that managers are able to relate to, and participate in, development work and take charge of work on readjustment.

- Constructive handling of internal and external conflicts.

- Continual, systematic work on improvements to environment, health and safety.

### Management and change

In relation to work on change, it is especially important to be aware of different managerial roles. It is obvious that very different challenges are associated with functioning as an elected leader, either political or professional (as in the university and college system), working in a secretariat for political leaders (such as a ministry), functioning on the board of a government agency and being a top manager or front-line manager in an agency. Development measures must as far as possible take account of both the distinctive features and the level of the institution. For example, in the university and college system, managers are elected for relatively short periods. Such knowledge institutions face special challenges in relation to responsibility for personnel and finances when administrative offices are held for a limited period of one to three years. Satisfactory management of such institutions and the safeguarding of the employer function require that elected administrators are provided with the necessary training.

Managerial tasks associated with organisational changes differ from those typical of stable operations. However, the need for continual improvement and adaptation of organisations is increasing. Readjustment often involves radical changes, such as new forms of association, downscaling of units, staff reductions and/or major re-orientations in relation to associates and users. Readjustment processes place considerable demands on personnel management, not least owing to the associated strain on employees.

Managerial groups often consist of sectoral managers who have varying access to information, different experiences and differing perceptions of any individual matter. The forms of communication and working methods within managerial groups are factors in the strategic readjustment and development of public bodies, and therefore play a major role in ensuring that readjustment processes are carried out constructively. Each member of the group is expected to identify with the overall purpose of the institution, while at the same time attending to his own sphere of responsibility. The balance between the parts and the whole is always a challenge for the management of an agency.

As a result of the complexity of public agencies and of the surrounding community, it is almost impossible for one person to handle all managerial tasks alone. Good teamwork, which is important during periods of stable operation, is therefore essential during periods of readjustment. It is therefore an advantage different members of the team to have different areas of expertise, so that they can attend to different functions, thereby complementing each other. Since such differences may lead to damaging conflicts, we stress the importance of conscious team-building.

During a readjustment process, a managerial group must continually assess whether the methods it employs enable it to tackle complex issues while safeguarding transparency and mutual trust between the managers in the group.

Guidance to both superiors and subordinates will always be an important task for managers in the Civil Service. However, professional briefings may be given too high a priority at the expense of other managerial tasks. Although Civil Service managers must be knowledgeable within their specialities, the roll of "superadviser" is fraught with pitfalls.

### 4. Example of leadership development programme

The Directorate of Public Management has been involved in development work both in the central government administration and in external agencies. Few systematic surveys have hitherto been made of the measures that have been carried out, the results that have been achieved or the experience that has been gained. During the plan period, priority will therefore be given to systematic assessment and documentation of the development measures. Impressions from previous work on manager development can be summarised as follows:

- Managers have varying awareness of their role as employer and varying involvement in questions concerning working environment, staff conflicts, competence-building and pay policy. There is a need to strengthen the employer function in the Civil Service. The new management pay agreement is an instrument designed to create a clearer employer role. The Department of Employer Affairs in the Ministry of Labour and Government Administration has also focused on the employer role by issuing a special discussion booklet.

- A conscious focus on management is needed in public agencies in order to raise the level of managerial competence.

- Managers are still wary of putting leadership issues on the agenda. This may be because they fear that this would be perceived as an admittance that they lack leadership competence. It is more likely that the opposite is the case: the best managers are those who are most preoccupied with developing their own skills.

- Development measures for managers must be differentiated in order to fulfil different, situational needs. Managers must therefore take responsibility themselves for ensuring the existence of adequate development measures.
- Managers must often lead activities that require political understanding and insight. This involves a need for follow-up, effective dialogue and reflection on experience.
- When dealing with difficult leadership dilemmas, many managers need the help of discussion partners and advisers.
- Experienced networks across ministries, levels and sectors have provided positive experience.
- Managers all say that they learn by sharing experience with other managers. Many agencies, though far from all, have prepared plans of action for competence-building that include managers. There is also a call for alternative career opportunities for managers as well as measures that make it simpler and more natural to alternate between the demanding role of manager and non-managerial posts.

There is a need for systematic assessment of the various development measures. The Ministry of Labour and Government Administration and the Directorate of Public Management will give this priority.

## 5. Women managers

In 1997, 22% of managers in central government administration were women. The proportion of women in top management was 12%. There are currently more highly educated and proficient female employees in the public administration than ever before. Yet there is still a clear under-representation of women in managerial posts in the Civil Service, although the statistics are better than in the private sector. The government's stated goal is to achieve a better gender balance. There is a clear need to make better use of the competence of female employees.

There are two major reasons for wanting to increase the number of women in senior administrative posts. Firstly, it is important that members of managerial teams have complementary managerial competence. Secondly, it is important to utilise the total managerial resources of an agency. The large group of highly qualified women offers considerable resources for both managerial posts and for posts requiring major professional expertise.

The main obstacles to increasing the proportion of female managers are attitudinal. Campaigns and individual measures have not shown sufficient success. There is a need for genuine, long-term measures at both central and local levels. The Ministry of Labour and Government Administration has therefore started the project "Women, Quality and Competence in the Civil Service". Agencies in all areas and at all levels of the administration have a responsibility for identifying and developing potential female managers.

The main strategies of the project are as follows:

- In co-operation with the other ministries, the Ministry of Labour and Government Administration has established a target in each sector for an increase in the number of women in top and middle management posts. These targets will be followed up through letters of allocation to external agencies, and linked to the performance requirements for individual managers. The ministries will submit annual reports to the Ministry of Labour and Government Administration.

- Establishment of a database containing details of appropriate female candidates for top managerial posts in the Civil Service.

- Planning of a separate mentoring programme for the government sector.

- Initiation of pilot projects involving agencies that wish to take active measures to increase the number of women in top and middle management posts.

- Assistance in disseminating research results, experience and other information.

- Development of R&D-based knowledge in the area of gender and competence, and initiating discussions on managerial roles and the recruiting of managers.

- The overall target is that the proportion of female managers in the Civil Service shall exceed 30% by the end of 2001.

## 6. Future developments

The most important products delivered by the Directorate of Public Management are competence development measures, guidance documents, consultancy and documentation in the form of analyses, assessments, etc. Efforts in management and manager development will be integrated with those in other areas, such as control and performance orientation, forms of organisation and readjustment, information technology and internationalisation. Within the framework drawn up in this document, the Directorate will ensure follow-up in the stated areas of focus in accordance with the management signals given by the ministry.

The direct consequences of this strategy document for the administration will mainly be decided by the individual agencies. Although, as a result of negotiations, some funds have been reserved for competence-building, and some of these funds have been applied to management development, the amount of resources reserved for improvement of managerial competence is decided by the individual agencies. The Ministry of Labour and Government Administration encourages the agencies to reserve adequate funds to implement the intentions of this strategy.

During the period of the strategy, the Ministry of Labour and Government Administration will give particular priority to measures that:

- result in more women in managerial posts;
- strengthen interaction across units and agencies;
- strengthen openness and transparency in the administration;
- strengthen continuous work on improvement of the Civil Service;
- improve managers' ability to deal with demanding readjustments and projects;
- help to develop the top management of the Civil Service;
- ensure documentation and assessment of development work.

# Chapter 7

# Leading Change in Mexico*

## 1. Introduction

On account of its background, the Mexican federal public administration has developed differently from those in most of the OECD countries. Its main characteristics are: total political group mobility and flexibility in the hiring and firing of middle and senior public servants; the existence of an informal career system (on average public servants stay in public administration twenty-five years, holding in this period several positions in different ministries or agencies); informal on the job cross-training due to high mobility; great flexibility to adapt to changes; and tenure for unionised public servants.

Even though an informal career system has operated with relative success in the federal public administration, circumstances – such as the high technical skills required nowadays for several positions in the federal public administration and the possibility of different political parties governing Mexico – has made it necessary to establish a career civil service that ensures a professional and politically neutral public administration.

A *new* approach (new in the Mexican political and historical context) necessitates an ambitious, overall reform process in public administration. The main goals are efficiency, efficacy and serving the population better. Needless to say, a tremendous inertia must be overcome in order to implant a new service culture, new processes and, in short, a whole new way of conducting public management. Success in this task requires knowledge, technical and political capacity, but especially a well constructed plan, based on an accurate diagnosis of the actual situation and identifying clear objectives.

The Ministry of Finance and the Comptroller General Office played leading roles in this process, while the human resource management (HRM) part of the reform process was taken in charge by the Civil Service Unit (USC) of the Ministry

---

* This paper was prepared and presented to the OECD HRM meeting in July 2000 by Mr. Luis Guillermo Ibarra, Head of the Civil Service Office, Ministry of Finance and Public Credit.

8⁶

of Finance. This office is empowered to regulate the federal civil service, to plan and keep control of the budget for HR and to authorise structural change within ministries and agencies in the Federal government.

## 2. Civil Service reform in Mexico

### General background

Mexican federal public administration is comprised of two types of employees: unionised (450 000 operational positions without considering teachers and doctors) and non-unionised (39 000 managerial positions). Due to the political relationship between the state and the unions, including the Federation of Unions of Federal Employees (FSTSE), unionised public servants enjoy the benefits of a special labour regime provided by the Federal Law for Workers at the Service of the State, while non-unionised public servants do not.

Thus, the law establishes a sort of career civil service scheme for unionised personnel, even though fraught with several problems in day-to-day operation, while for more than 70 years the lack of a specific legal regime applicable to middle and senior public servants has prevented the establishment of a federal civil service.

In the Mexican federal public administration, there were no formal processes for recruitment and selection, or professional development. Personal capacities of candidates were more important than objective technical criteria for fitting the job description, and political favouritism also affected the recruitment and develop-ment of experienced personnel.

Income of public servants was not related to job evaluation or performance appraisal. Salaries were fixed according to hierarchy and did not recognise differences in responsibility, complexity, or risk. There was also an unreasonable flexibility in bonuses (merit pay) which created further inequities and fostered personal rather than institutional loyalties among public servants. In addition, there were five different income groups, reflecting the political capacity of some ministries and agencies to obtain more economic resources.

Training was granted only to unionised public servants. Middle and senior public servants did not attend training courses because continuity in their functions was regarded as essential. For this reason, sometimes middle and senior public servants were unable to acquire new technical tools and administrative skills that would help them improve their managerial and decision-making capacities. Furthermore, federal government was not legally obliged to provide training to non-unionised public servants.

## Constructing a federal Civil Service

The Civil Service Unit (USC) was mandated to carry out the task of constructing a federal Civil Service that would improve efficiency in Mexican public administration. However, the USC lacked a coherent organisation and the operational capacity to carry out its mandate. It had cumbersome procedures for decision-making, an absence of regulations on HRM, and operating procedures. There was also very little communication between the divisions within the USC; information was concentrated in a few persons, thus creating power enclaves in the organisation.

In 1995 the USC set up a research team in order to gather information on the civil service systems operating in America and overseas. By 1996, the research team had developed a model for the Mexican federal public administration which included the following revisions.

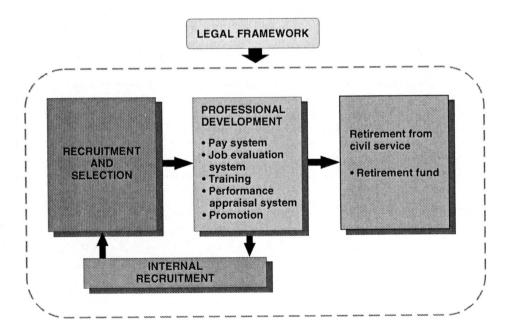

*Source:* OECD.

## Pay scale and bonuses

One of the first steps taken by the USC was to restructure the compensation system (salaries, bonuses, and fringe benefits) to make it more transparent, fair and competitive. A new pay scale was begun in 1995 with salary bands in each hierarchical level gradually implemented. In the year 2000, this enabled the implementation of a flexible pay scale divided into hierarchical groups, responsibility grades (according to job evaluation) and salary levels. The lack of transparency in the compensation system generated by bonuses was also modified to ensure that bonuses and fringe benefits become transparent and equitable.

These changes in the compensation system required downsizing the federal public administration in order to cover its additional budget cost. Ministries and agencies were required to reduce by 30% the cost of the payroll of middle and senior public servants. Several regulations were issued in order to induce savings in ministries and agencies.

The new compensation system is clearly set down in the *Pay and Benefits Handbook for Middle and Senior Public Servants of the Federal Public Administration* issued in January 2000. For the first time a modern system allows hierarchical, responsibility grade and salary level promotions, determined through a job evaluation system, which will facilitate the operation of a merit-based civil service for the Mexican federal public administration.

*Performance appraisal*

In March 2000, the Ministry of Finance issued the regulation that established the guidelines for the performance appraisal of federal public servants. These guidelines provided a general framework to be followed by all ministries and agencies in the establishment of their particular performance appraisal systems. The systems were to be put into effect by July 2000 to allow ministries and agencies to award bonuses and salary level promotions to their public servants. These will not only allow the objective evaluation of personnel, but should also help to assess training requirements. Evaluations will have to be made at least twice a year. An important innovation is that the evaluation in some cases will be made not only by the public servant's superior, but also by his/her peers and subordinates (*i.e.* a 360-degree feedback).

*Training*

From 1996 to 1999, the USC worked on establishing the bases to make training compulsory for middle and senior public servants. In July 2000, the regulation establishing the general training scheme for the federal public servants was issued.

The training system is divided into three stages: training requirements assessment (in which the performance appraisal system is used); training development (linked to job requirements) and training evaluation and monitoring.

The training regulation will ensure the provision of training to all the hierarchical levels of the federal public administration. This is a breakthrough in the Mexican federal public administration, because, as explained above, training was offered only on a non-regular basis to operational levels (the lower echelons of the hierarchical structure).

Furthermore for the first time, training results will be evaluated and used with the purpose of improving the training programmes and measuring their overall impact in the ministries' service delivery. This will allow the identification of opportunity areas for course programming. It is expected not only to strengthen professional development, but also to increase the productivity, efficiency and responsiveness of the federal government's organisations.

## Database

The Unified Information System (SIARH) was also created during the reform process. SIARH is a human resource database accessible to all ministries and agencies of the federal government. A National Affiliation System now gathers information such as: general data; education; training, performance appraisal and promotions records of each federal public servant. Additionally, it serves as a vacancy database for all ministries and agencies that will allow placing laid off public servants in new posts. The Human Resources Budget Integration System speeds up processes of integration, execution and follow-up of the global budget for human resources of the federal government. Finally, the Organisational Structures System, allows automatic registration of structural changes within ministries and identifies the public servant holding each post in the federal public administration.

## 3. Leading change – an example of leadership

### The importance of leadership

The process of constructing the steps towards the establishment of a federal Civil Service had to overcome several difficulties threatening the capacity of the USC to lead the change. Modifying the prevailing organisational culture in the federal public administration implied a complex leadership strategy, that required first changing the USC's own organisational culture, in order to be able to lead the HR reform credibly. In addition, its actions and changes, because they would not only affect the ministries and agencies operation, but its people, had to be legitimated at the highest level. To accomplish this task the President, through the Ministry of Finance, had to persuade Congress to incorporate regulations in the Budget Decree that would give support, and share the responsibility of the actions taken.

### Leadership strategies

Redesigning the structure of the USC and changing the organisational and labour culture of all its employees in order to lead the HRM reform process was achieved through the implantation of a quality assurance system (QS). This has helped to develop a new service culture within USC's organisation, where satisfying clients' needs and expectations have become the main objective.

For the first time in its history, the USC has had to define clearly its mission, vision, quality policies and the basic performance principles of the organisation. This required the creation of the Directive Committee on Quality (DCQ) in which USC's senior public servants participated. (*i.e.* the Head of the USC, along with the Assistant Director Generals and the Directors).

Once these basic steps were achieved, it was necessary to create conscious-ness in the USC's personnel of the mission, vision and the importance of improving the quality of the services provided. In order to achieve this task, the Head of the USC met with the unit's personnel (340 people) to explain the system purpose and persuade public servants to assume an active role in reaching this ambitious goal. In addition, the former president of the National Quality Award (private sector oriented quality award), was invited to deliver a lecture on the benefits of total quality management to bring an external perspective and motivate the personnel.

To be able to implement the policy decisions defined by the DCQ and have a permanent link with the USC's operating areas, an Executive Committee on Quality (ECQ), was established with the participation of all the middle public servants (*i.e.* Directors, Deputy Directors and Department Heads). The ECQ's main function is to design the programme for the implementation of the quality policies defined by the DCQ. After the approval of the programme by the DCQ, the ECQ is in charge of implementing it, with the help of specific working groups comprising the public servants who intervene in the process being reviewed, regardless of their hierarchical level. The working groups are the cells of the quality structure: through them, the DCQ receives feedback on the feasibility of the policies defined and they have been the best way of addressing people's desires and expectations towards their work.

Both DCQ and ECQ worked on the identification of opportunity areas for improvement, which included the assessment of resources required for service provisions. Later, public servants at every level of the organisation had to learn to work as a team and participate in putting in writing the operational procedures, and to review the regulations in order to deregulate and cut red tape. The Head of the USC actively participated in the implementation of the QS, and still does when it is required.

As a result of the procedure review, requirements for service provision were clearly defined and deregulated, thus allowing the setting of a controlled response time for each process. Service guides were issued, in order to further understanding in ministries and agencies of requirements for obtaining authorisa-tion. Responsibility for authorising has been devolved, and public servants in the lower echelons of the organisation have been empowered to make decisions. The implementation of the QS has helped to identify and develop natural leaders at all levels of the organisation.

In most cases, these persons have been appointed by the Assistant General Directors as ISO change agents, whose task is to facilitate, monitor and make recommendations on the performance of QS. At present, the Head of the Unit monitors the response times and quality of the services provided, in order to be able to anticipate measures to keep them within the defined ranges. Along with the Assistant General Directors, he also visits the areas on a regular basis to assess the prevailing labour environment, as well as to verify that the quality policies are being followed and to get firsthand feedback on personnel expectations and needs.

It is important to point out that the QS has helped to evaluate the leadership skills of Directors and Deputy Directors and Department Heads, given that a healthy competition has developed between the USC's operative areas. This has oriented the way leadership-training courses have to be provided and alerted the DCQ to concentrate on those middle public servants who show weaker leading capacity.

By 1997 it was clear that the QS was working properly so the DCQ decided to register all the processes and services that were delivered under the quality assurance standards of the International Standards Organization (ISO). To make this more challenging, the ISO 9001 standard was chosen. This is the most difficult standard to conform to, because it covers the whole process of production of goods and services, from their design to delivery. Needless to say, there are very few private sector companies in Mexico and throughout the world that are able to certify the conformance of their QS with this standard.

In July 1999 USC got its QS registered by the Quality Management Institute of Canada, which is the leading registration organisation in North America and also chairs the IQNet, a network of 28 registration organisations of different countries. With the available information, this makes the USC the only federal government office in the world that has a full certification of all its services and processes under the ISO 9001 standard.

At present USC is working on producing a simplified guide on quality assurance systems implantation in public sector organisations. This document is intended to help ministries and agencies to implement QS as a way to improve governments' responsiveness to people.

## 4. Conclusion

One of the most daring challenges in a reform process appears when the administrative unit that is supposed to lead the change is outranked by those who require its services. That was the case of the USC, and of other budget planning

9

offices at the Ministry of Finance, where the public servants who required their services held higher posts than those of the heads of these offices.

Although controlling the budget wields a great amount of power over ministries and agencies, it is important for those who control it to legitimate their decisions and actions, in order not to create political conflict and be able to lead change. In this sense, the actions taken by the USC to improve the quality of its service and show transparency and fairness in the way decisions that affect ministries and agencies are made, have given credibility to the organisation and have helped avoid unnecessary confrontation, thus allowing the implementation of the measures mentioned above.

The USC and areas in charge of HRM in the federal public administration will be issuing the regulation that establishes the general training scheme. It has been necessary to meet with the areas in charge of HRM in all the ministries and agencies and to persuade them of the importance of improving training programmes and locks have been established in the federal budget to safeguard the use of resources for training. In addition, the Comptroller-General office has established a mechanism to assess the effectiveness of resources invested for training purposes.

It is important to mention that the HRM reform process had to offer benefits also for unionised personnel if it was to succeed. For this reason, since the beginning of President Zedillo's administration several measures were taken to improve their income, with the agreement of FSTSE. A new fringe benefit was created as an incentive to support training and personal skills development of unionised workers. In addition, the regulation for performance appraisal was reviewed and improved, to make it compulsory for the assessment of training needs of this type of personnel.

Nowadays, in order to be able to regulate and establish a recruitment and selection system for federal personnel, including middle and senior public servants, a trial programme is being implemented on a voluntary basis in seven ministries. For this purpose, each ministry has chosen the offices where it is to be applied. This will require that the offices define the requirements for each of their posts, and elaborate the selection exams and the administrative procedures for job assignment. If the trial programme is successful, it will be implemented in the federal public administration.

*Appendix*

# Executive Core Qualifications

## Leading change

*Continual learning* – Grasps the essence of new information; masters new technical and business knowledge; recognises own strengths and weaknesses; pursues self-development; seeks feedback from others and opportunities to master new knowledge.

*Creativity and innovation* – Develops new insights into situations and applies innovative solutions to make organisational improvements; creates a work environment that encourages creative thinking and innovation; designs and implements new or cutting-edge programmes/processes.

*External awareness* – Identifies and keeps up-to-date on key national and international policies and economic, political and social trends that affect the organisations. Understands short-term and long-range plans and determines how best to be positioned to achieve a competitive business advantage in a global economy.

*Flexibility* – Is open to change and new information: adapts behaviour and work methods in response to new information; changing conditions, or unexpected obstacles. Adjusts rapidly to new situations warranting attention and resolution.

*Resilience* – Deals effectively with pressure; maintains focus and intensity and remains optimistic and persistent, even under adversity. Recovers quickly from setbacks. Effectively balances personal life and work.

*Service motivation* – Creates and sustains an organisational culture which encourages others to provide the quality of service essential to high performance. Enables others to acquire the tools and support they need to perform well. Shows a commitment to public service. Influences others toward a spirit of service and meaningful contributions to mission accomplishment.

*Strategic thinking* – Formulates effective strategies consistent with the business and competitive strategy of the organisation in a global economy. Examines policy issues and strategic planning with a long-term perspective. Determines objectives and sets priorities; anticipates potential threats or opportunities.

*Vision* – Takes a long-term view and acts as a catalyst for organisational change; builds a shared vision with others. Persuades others to translate vision into action.

## Leading people

*Conflict management* – Identifies and takes steps to prevent unpleasant confrontations. Manages and resolves conflicts and disagreements in a positive and constructive manner.

9

---

*Cultural awareness* – Initiates and manages cultural change to the benefit of the organisation. Values cultural diversity and other individual differences in the workforce. Ensures that the organisation builds on these differences and that employees are treated in a fair and equitable manner.

*Integrity/honesty* – Instils mutual trust and confidence; creates a culture that fosters high standards of ethics; behaves in a fair and ethical manner towards others, and demonstrates a sense of corporate responsibility and commitment to public service.

*Team building* – Inspires, motivates, and guides others toward goal accomplishments. Consistently develops and sustains co-operative working relationships. Encourages and facilitates co-operation within the organisation and with customer groups; fosters commitment, team spirit, pride, trust. Develops leadership in others through coaching, mentoring, rewarding, and guiding employees.

## Results driven

*Accountability* – Assures that effective controls are developed and maintained to ensure the integrity of the organisation. Holds self and others accountable for rules and responsibilities. Can be relied upon to ensure that projects within areas of specific responsibility are completed in a timely manner and within budget. Monitors and evaluates plans; focuses on results and measuring attainment of outcomes.

*Customer service* – Balancing interests of a variety of clients; readily readjusts priorities to respond to pressing and changing client demands. Anticipates and meets the need of clients; achieves quality end-products; is committed to continuous improvement of services.

*Decisiveness* – Exercises good judgement by making sound and well-informed decisions, perceives the impact and implications of decisions; makes effective and timely decisions, even when data are limited or solutions produce unpleasant consequences; is proactive and achievement-oriented.

*Entrepreneurship* – Identifies opportunities to develop and market new products and services within or outside of the organisation. Is willing to take risks; initiates actions that involve a deliberate risk to achieve a recognised benefit or advantage.

*Problem solving* – Identifies and analyses problems; distinguishes between relevant and irrelevant information to make logical decisions; provides solutions to individual and organisational problems.

*Technical credibility* – Understands and appropriately applies procedures, requirements, regulations, and policies related to specialised expertise. Is able to make sound hiring and capital resources decisions to address training and development needs. Understands linkages between administrative competencies and mission needs.

## Business acumen

*Financial management* – Demonstrates broad understanding of principles of financial management and marketing expertise necessary to ensure appropriate funding levels. Prepares, justifies, and/or administers the budget for the programme area; uses cost-benefit thinking to set priorities; monitors expenditures in support of programmes and policies. Identifies cost-effective approaches. Manages procurement and contracting.

*Human resources management* – Assesses current and future staffing needs based on organisational goals and budget realities. Using merit principles, ensures staff are appropriately selected, developed, utilised, appraised and rewarded; takes corrective action.

*Technology management* – Uses efficient and cost-effective approaches to integrate technology into the workplace and improve programme effectiveness. Develops strategies using new technology to enhance decision making. Understands the impact of technological changes on the organisation.

### Building coalitions and communications

*Influencing/negotiating* – Persuades others; builds consensus through give and take; gains co-operation from others to obtain information and accomplish goals; facilitates "win-win" situations.

*Interpersonal skills* – Considers and responds appropriately to the needs, feelings, and capabilities of different people in different situations; is tactful, compassionate and sensitive, and treats others with respect.

*Oral communication* – Makes clear and convincing oral presentations to individuals or groups; listens effectively and clarifies information as needed; facilitates an open exchange of ideas and fosters an atmosphere of open communication.

*Partnering* – Develops networks and builds alliances, engages in cross-functional activities; collaborates across boundaries, and finds common ground with a widening range of stakeholders. Utilises contacts to build and strengthen internal support bases.

*Political savvy* – Identifies the internal and external politics that have an impact on the work of the organisation. Approaches each problem situation with a clear perception of organisational and political reality; recognises the impact of alternative courses of action.

*Written communication* – Expresses facts and ideas in writing in a clear, convincing and organised manner.

OECD PUBLICATIONS, 2, rue André-Pascal, 75775 PARIS CEDEX 16
PRINTED IN FRANCE
(42 2001 12 1 P) ISBN 92-64-19529-7 – No. 52095 2001

Printed in the United States
65108LVS00002B/43-44